THE MICHAEL MYSTERY

RUDOLF STEINER

Translated by
Marjorie Spock

NOTE

Faithfully translated by Marjorie Spock from the original texts of Rudolf Steiner's Letters *To The Members* and their accompanying Guidelines which appeared weekly in *Was in der Anthroposophischen Gesellschaft vorgeht, Nachrichten für deren Mitglieder* Members' Supplement to *Das Goetheanum* from August 17, 1924 to April 12, 1925.

In the Collected Edition of Rudolf Steiner's works, the volume containing the German texts is entitled *Anthroposophische Leitsätze* (Vol. 26 in the Bibliographic Survey, 1961).

Copyright © 1984 by Marjorie Spock

CONTENTS

I

AT THE DAWNING OF THE AGE OF MICHAEL

Prior to the ninth century after the Mystery of Golgotha, men had a different relationship to their thoughts than they had later on. They did not feel that the thoughts that lived within their souls were their own product, but regarded them rather as gifts given them by the spiritual world. Even such thoughts as they entertained about what they perceived with their senses seemed to them revelations of the divine, conveyed by objects in the sense world.

Anyone able to perceive the spirit understands this feeling.

A person to whom a spiritual reality is manifested never feels that the spiritual percept is given and that the perceiving person forms the concept· whereby he grasps it. It is rather a case of actually *seeing* the thought contained in the percept, a thought just as objectively present as is the percept itself.

During the ninth century—this is, of course, only an approximate time, to be understood as a median; the transition took place gradually—individual personal intelligence began to illumine the souls of human beings. People got the feeling that *they formed* their thoughts. This thought-forming activity became the predominant feature of soul life, so that thinkers conceived of the human soul as expressing itself fundamentally in the application of intelligence. The previous conception of the soul had been an imaginative one. The soul's nature was seen as participating in the content of the spiritual world rather than as active thought-formation. Supersensible spiritual beings were thought of as engaged in thinking and working on man, and sending in their thoughts into him as well. This content of the supersensible spiritual world living in man was felt to be the soul.

1

We encounter concrete spiritual beings immediately upon penetrating the spiritual realm with clairvoyant vision. In ancient teachings, the being from whom the thoughts bound up with things flow forth was called Michael. We can retain the name here. So it can be said that people once received the thoughts that came to them from Michael. Michael ruled over cosmic intelligence.

From the ninth century onward, human beings no longer felt that Michael was inspiring their thoughts. Thoughts had fallen away from his dominion; they descended from the spiritual world into the individual souls of men.

From then on, the life of thought was nurtured by the human race. At first, uncertainty reigned as to what people were dealing with in the thoughts they had. Scholastic doctrine reflects this uncertainty. There were two categories of these philosophers: Realists and Nominalists.

The Realists, led by Thomas Aquinas and his fellow-thinkers, still sensed the ancient unity between thoughts and things. They therefore saw in thought a reality living in the object; they conceived of a person's thoughts as realities that flowed from out of things into the souls of those who perceived them. —

The Nominalists were keenly aware of the fact that souls formed their own thoughts. They felt thoughts to be a purely subjective element that lived in the soul but had nothing to do with things themselves. In their view, thoughts were mere names that people made up for things. (They spoke not of 'thoughts' but of 'universals,' but this does not affect the principle they upheld, since thoughts always have a universal connotation in their relationship to things.)

We could say: The Realists wanted to keep faith with Michael. Then, too, in view of the fact that thoughts had descended from Michael's realm into that of man, they wanted their thinking to serve him as the lord of cosmic intelligence. — The Nominalists, however, carried to completion, on a subconscious soul level, the falling away from Michael. They regarded man rather than Michael as the possessor of thoughts. Nominalism gained ground and influence.—This was the situation up to the last third of the nineteenth century, a period during which individuals able to perceive spiritual events in the universe felt that Michael remained connected with the stream of intellectual life. He seeks a new metamorphosis of his cosmic task. In earlier times, he allowed thoughts to stream from the external spiritual world into human souls. Beginning with the last third of the nineteenth century, it is his desire to live *in* human souls as thoughts are formed there. In that earlier age, human beings who were related to Michael perceived him carrying on his activity in the realm of the spirit. Now they realize that they must allow him to live in their hearts. They now dedicate their thought-nourished spiritual life to him. In their independent individual life of thought, they let Michael teach them the paths their souls should be following.

Individuals who, in their former earthly lives, were recipients of inspired thoughts—individuals who, in other words, served Michael—felt themselves drawn to voluntary participation in the community of Michael upon reentering earthly incarnation at the end of the nineteenth century. From now on, they regarded the olden inspirer of their thinking as their guide in higher thought activity.

A person alert to such matters could perceive what a transformation occurred in the thought life of the human race during the last third of the nineteenth century. Prior to that time, a person could only feel that thoughts were formed by his own activity. Beginning with the period cited, he can rise above himself and project his awareness into spiritual realms. There he encounters Michael, who reveals himself as linked from olden times with all thought activity. He frees thoughts from their restriction to the head region and opens a way for them to the heart. He sets inner enthusiasm glowing, enabling man to give himself in soul devotion to everything that can be experienced in the light of thought. The Michael Age has arrived. Hearts are beginning to have thoughts. Enthusiasm is no longer generated by obscure mysticism, but by inner clarity supported by thoughts. To grasp this is to receive Michael into one's inner being. Thoughts that aim at understanding matters of the spirit in our time must spring from hearts devoted to Michael as the fiery cosmic lord of thought.

*

GUIDELINES

1. One can approach the third hierarchy (Archai, Archangels, Angels) in spirit if one comes to know thinking, feeling and willing as the manifestation of the spirit's activity within the soul. Thinking creates mere images, not reality. Feeling has a weaving life in this pictorial element; it calls attention to a reality in man but cannot live it out. Willing produces a reality that, though it presupposes the possession of a body, does not share consciously in its shaping. The actual being that lives in thinking to render the body the instrument of that thinking; the actual being that lives in feeling to make the body a fellow-participant in the experiencing of a reality and the actual being that lives in will activity to share consciously in its shaping, has its life in the third hierarchy.

2. One can approach the second hierarchy (Kyriotetes, Dynameis, Exusiai) in spirit when one sees, in the facts of nature, phenomena produced by a spiritual element *living* within them. The second hierarchy thus has nature as its dwelling place in order to work on souls from within it.

3. One can approach the first hierarchy (Seraphim, Cherubim, Thrones) in spirit when one perceives the facts of the natural and human kingdoms to be deeds (creations) of a spiritual element at work in them. The first hierarchy, then, has the kingdoms of man and nature as the locus of its activity, in which it carries out what in it lies.

4

II
MAN'S SOUL STATE PRIOR TO
THE DAWNING OF THE MICHAEL AGE

The Age of Michael dawned in human evolution after a period in which, on the one hand, intellectual thought activity predominated, while, on the other, man's gaze was focused on the external physical world of the senses.

The forming of thoughts is *not* intrinsically a development in the direction of materialism. The world of ideas, which made itself known to man in earlier times in the form of inspiration, became an individual soul possession in the period prior to the Michael Age. No longer did souls receive ideas 'from above' as the content of the spiritual world. They now actively drew them forth from their own spirits. This step represents a maturing to the point where man became able to reflect on his own spiritual essence. Previously, he never penetrated to the depth of his own being. He regarded himself rather as a drop separated out of the sea of spiritual being for the period of his earthly life, to return at its conclusion to that ocean.

The thought-forming activity taking place within man represents an advance in his self-knowledge. To the supersensible view, matters stand as follows: the spiritual powers to which we may assign the name of Michael had dominion over ideas in the spiritual universe. Man experienced these ideas as he participated in the life of Michael's realm. He now experiences them as his own, with the result that he has been separated for the time being from the Michaelic world. The inspired thoughts of earlier days brought him the content of the spiritual world as well. But as inspiration ceased to flow and individuals began actively forming their own thoughts, man had to turn to sensory perception to find a content for his thoughts. This meant temporarily filling with a material content the personal spirit to which he had attained. He fell into a materialistic way of looking at things in the epoch that brought his own spirit to a level higher than the one that preceded it.

This situation can easily be misunderstood. One may note only the fall into materialism and be saddened by it. But while the *outlook* of this period had to restrict itself to the external physical world, there developed in the soul's depths a *purified, independent human spirituality as experience.* In the Michael Age, this spirituality may no longer remain unconscious *experience*; it must become conscious of its real nature, and that signifies the entrance of the Michael being into human souls. For a certain period of time, man filled his own spirit with material views of the natural world. Now he is to fill it again with a spirituality truly his own, as cosmic content.

For a time, thought-forming lost itself to material aspects of the cosmos. Now it must find itself again in the cosmic spirit. Warmth and spirituality, permeated with essential being, can flow into the cold, abstract thought world. This characterizes the dawn of the Michael Age.

Only in separation from the thought being of the cosmos could a consciousness of freedom develop in the depths of human souls. What had its origin in the heights had to be discovered anew from out of the depths. That is why the development of this consciousness of freedom had to be based temporarily on a natural science that focused its attention exclusively on externals. During the period in which man was unconsciously readying his spirit for pure ideas, his senses were focused outward on the material, a realm that did not impinge in any way on the delicate seed growing up within him.

But an experiencing of the spiritual and, coupled with it, spiritual perception itself, can enter again in a new way into contemplation of external matter. The knowledge of nature acquired under the sign of materialism can be grasped in its spiritual aspect in the soul's inwardness. Michael, who once spoke 'from above,' can be heard speaking 'from within,' where he has taken up his new abode. We might say, to put it more imaginatively, that the sun element that man absorbed for so long only from the cosmos will begin shining in the soul itself. People will learn to speak of an 'inner sun.' This will not cause man to feel less a being of the earth in his life between birth and death, but he will know himself to be *sun-guided* on his earthly course. He will come to feel how true it is that a being illumines him inwardly with a light that, though it shines upon earthly existence, is not lit there. As the Age of Michael dawns, it may seen as though all this were still remote from human experience. Spiritually, however, it is near; it need only be 'seen.' It is immeasurably important that men's ideas should not stop at being merely 'thought,' but should go on to become 'seeing' in the thinking of them.

*

GUIDELINES

1. Man of the present period experiences himself in waking day-consciousness. This experience conceals the fact that within his 'awakeness' the third hierarchy is present in his experiencing.

2. In the consciousness of dreaming, man has a chaotic experience of his own being inharmoniously united with the spiritual being of the cosmos. If this dream consciousness is replaced with its opposite pole, imaginative consciousness, he becomes aware that the second hierarchy is present in his experiencing.

3. In dreamless sleep, man experiences without self-awareness the union of his own being with the spiritual being of the world. If sleeping consciousness is replaced by its op-

posite pole, inspired consciousness, he becomes aware that the first hierarchy is present in his experiencing.

III

THE PRE-MICHAELIC AND THE MICHAELIC PATH

We will not form the correct concept of Michael's influence on mankind's evolution as long as we conceive the relationship of the world of ideas to Nature in the way it is ordinarily conceived today.

According to that way of thinking, Nature, with its creatures and processes, is outside us, ideas inside. These ideas are concepts of what Nature has created, or of what we call the laws of Nature. Thinkers are primarily concerned here with showing how we form the particular ideas that relate to things of Nature or embody natural laws.

This reflects scant concern for the way these ideas are related to the man who has them. But if we are to understand the matter, we must ask the all-important question, "What is man experiencing as he entertains the scientific ideas of recent times?"

An answer is to be found in the following consideration.

At present, man feels that ideas are formed in him by his own soul activity. He senses that he is the shaper of ideas, and that only his perceptions come to him from outside himself.

People did not always have this feeling. In earlier times, the content of ideas was felt to be received as a gift from the supersensible world rather than as something produced by oneself.

This feeling underwent several evolutionary stages depending on how man experienced what we now call ideas with the different parts of his being. In our present epoch, the age of the development of the consciousness soul, the situation is exactly as described in the previous Guidelines:

"Thoughts have their actual seat in man's etheric body. But there they are forces endowed with life and being. They imprint themselves upon the physical body and exist there in the shadowy form in which ordinary consciousness knows them."

We can project ourselves back into times in which thoughts were experienced directly in the ego. At that time they were anything but shadowy. Not only were they filled with *life*, they were also ensouled and spirit-permeated. But this is to say that man was not a thinker of thoughts, but rather that he perceived and experienced spiritual beings.

We find this awareness of a world of spiritual beings in all the peoples of antiquity. Remnants of it that have come down to us in history are referred to as the myth-making state of mind, and no great importance is attached to it for an understanding of the real world.—Yet, human beings in that state of consciousness were at home in *their own* world, the world of their origin, whereas, in the consciousness of present times, they are lifted out of it.

Man is a spirit, and *his* world is the world of spirits.

The next level is one of an experience of thought in the astral body rather than in the ego. To the soul view, spirituality is no longer immediately perceptible there; the thought element appears as ensouled life.

On the first level, that of an immediate view of concrete spiritual beings, man does not feel a very strong need to apply what he thus perceives to the world perceptible to his physical senses. Sense phenomena do indeed reveal themselves to be the product of what is spiritually perceived, but he is not moved to develop a special science of what lies immediately open to the eyes of the spirit. Then, too, the view of the world of spiritual beings thus beheld is one of such fullness as to hold first claim on his attention.

This changes on his reaching the second level of consciousness. The concrete spiritual beings withdraw from sight, but their radiance makes itself felt as ensouled life.

10

Man begins to relate the 'life of nature' to this 'life of soul,' seeking in the creations and processes of nature the spiritual beings whose activity produced them. The imprint of this state of consciousness is to be found historically in the alchemistic striving that appeared on the scene in the later stages of that state.

On the first level of consciousness, man lived wholly *in his own being* when he 'thought' spiritual beings. On the second level, he was still fairly close to himself and to his origin.

This means that, on both levels, there could be no real question of his having personal, inner motives for his actions.

A spirituality to which he was akin acted in him. What *he* seemed to be doing was a manifestation of processes originating in spiritual beings. His actions were sense-perceptible revelations of what an actual spiritual world was bringing about.

A third epoch in the evolution of consciousness produced thoughts, but they were alive and came to awareness in the etheric body.

When Greek civilization was at its peak, it lived in this consciousness. When Greeks thought, they were not producing thoughts whereby they perceived the world as though with a tool of their own making; rather did they feel life come alive in them, the same life that pulsed in objects and processes around them.

That was the moment that witnessed the birth of a longing for personal freedom of action. Not that actual freedom was born at that moment, but simply the longing to experience it.

An individual, experiencing the stirring life of Nature as a force stirring in himself as well, now became able to develop the longing to separate his inner life from that about him, for he now felt it to be an alien element. But this external life was still felt to be the last product of an active spiritual world similar to that to which man himself belonged.

Only when thoughts left their imprint on the physical body and consciousness extended only to the perception of those imprints did freedom become possible. That is the state of affairs arrived at in the fifteenth century, A.D.

The import that contemporary ideas of Nature may have for Nature itself is not what matters in the world's evolution, for these ideas did not take the form they have assumed in order to supply a particular picturing of Nature, but rather for the purpose of bringing human beings to a particular stage of development.

When thoughts laid hold on the physical body, then spirit, soul and life were driven out of them, leaving only the abstract shadows that cling to the physical instrument. Thoughts of this kind cannot do other than make physical-material things the object of knowledge; their only *reality* lies in their connection with man's physical-material body.

Materialism came into being, not because there is nothing to be perceived in outer nature except material beings and processes, but because it was necessary for man to go through an evolutionary stage that brought him to a state of consciousness capable of focusing on matter only. The one-sided development of this human evolutionary need resulted in the natural-scientific outlook of the present day.

It is Michael's mission to bring into human ether bodies the forces whereby men's shadowy thoughts are re-enlivened. Soul-spiritual beings of the world beyond the senses will incline themselves to these quickened thoughts. In his new freedom, man will be able to live in them as they were once lived in by men of old who were merely the physical reflection of *their* activity.

*

GUIDELINES

1. In the course of humanity's evolution, consciousness has descended the ladder of thought development rung by rung. On the first level, man experienced thoughts in his ego as spirit-permeated, ensouled, life-endowed beings. On the

second level, he experienced them in his astral body where they reflect only soul and life aspects of these spiritual beings. On the third level, he experienced them in his ether body; there they presented themselves only as inner stirrings of life reminiscent of the soul element. On the contemporary fourth level, thoughts are experienced in the physical body as dead shadows of the spirit.

2. To the same degree that the spiritual, soul and life aspects of human thinking withdraw, man's individual will comes into the ascendant; freedom becomes possible.

3. It is the mission of Michael to lead man upward again, on the path of his will, to those realms from which he descended when, on the path of thinking, his earth-consciousness underwent a transformation from a supersensible to a physical way of experiencing.

IV
MICHAEL'S TASK IN THE AHRIMANIC REALM

If we look back in spirit over the last five centuries of human development, noting the particular aspects that man's inner life has assumed in that time period, we *must* have at least some inkling, in our ordinary consciousness, of the fact that these centuries have brought him to a highly significant turning point in his whole earthly evolution.

In the previous issue of the Newsletter, I called attention to this important turning point from one particular angle. We can look back over earlier periods of evolution and see what a transformation the soul faculty, presently functioning as intelligence, has undergone.

At the present time, thoughts of a dead, abstract nature make their appearance on the stage of consciousness. They are tied to the physical body of man. He has to acknowledge them as his own product.

When a man of primal times turned his attention in the direction in which he presently becomes aware of his own thoughts, he perceived instead divine-spiritual beings. He knew his whole existence, even his physical body, to be bound up with these beings, and he had to recognize *himself* as their creation. And not only this. He saw his *actions*, too, as being of their prompting. He had no such thing as a will of his own. What he did was the manifestation of divine willing.

Step by step, as described previously, and beginning about five centuries ago, individual will came into its own.

The final step differs more sharply, however, from those that preceded it than do any of these others from one another.

Thoughts lose their livingness upon entering a relationship with the physical body; they become dead, spiritually dead structures. In earlier times, when they were man's inner possession, they were also still organs of the divine-spiritual beings with whom man was united. They *willed* in him as *living beings*. And through them man felt himself livingly linked to the spiritual world.

With the advent of dead thoughts, he feels himself separated from the spiritual world and transposed wholly into the physical.

But this means he is transposed into the sphere of Ahriman's mentality, which is relatively powerless in those realms where the beings of the higher hierarchies kept man in *their* sphere, either by carrying on their activity directly in him as they did in antiquity, or, later on, through the agency of their living and ensouled reflection. As long as this activity of supersensible beings continued to work over into human functioning—and this was the case up until about the fifteenth century—Ahrimanic forces had only a minimal influence on human development.

The picture of Ahriman's activity, presented as the old Persians conceived it, does not contradict this statement. The Persians had in mind, not a working of Ahriman in human soul development, but rather his activity in the world bordering immediately on the human soul world. Although Ahriman's machinations make themselves felt as something emanating from a neighboring spiritual realm and playing over into the human soul world, they have no direct effect upon it.

Direct encroachment became possible only with the advent of the past five centuries.

At this point, man reached the end of an evolutionary stream that has made him the product of divine mentality that *gave up its own* nature in order to become abstract intelligence in him.

Man did not remain in the realms in which he had his origin as a product of that divine mind.

The evolution that took place in human *consciousness* five centuries ago had already taken place in man's *overall* development at the time when the Mystery of Golgotha occurred. The great majority of humankind was unaware that man's evolution had gradually descended from a sphere in which Ahriman was relatively powerless into one where he was a much stronger force. This gradual slipping down onto a different world level came to a conclusion in the fifteenth century.

It is possible for Ahriman to gain influence over man on this world level and to wreak havoc there because it is just on this level that the divine activity from which man sprang has died away. But there was no other way for man to develop free will than by entering a sphere where the divine-spiritual beings, to whom he was related from the time of his origin no longer lived.

Looked at from a cosmic standpoint, the sun mystery can be discerned in the way human evolution took its course. The divine-spiritual beings of man's origin were present in what he was able to perceive in the sun up to the time when the above significant turning point in his development took place. *These* beings separated from the sun, leaving on it only their extinct remains, with the result that he could henceforth receive from the sun and incorporate into his bodily being only the capacity to form dead thoughts.

But it was these same beings who sent the Christ down from the sun onto the earth, and for mankind's redemption, Christ has united *His* being with the dead remnant of divine-spiritual being in Ahriman's kingdom. This has given humanity that twofold possibility that is the guarantee of freedom: to turn to the Christ, this time consciously, in the spiritual attitude of mind unconsciously present during the period of man's descent from immediate perception of supersensible reality to the application of intelligence, or else to luxuriate in a personal sense of release from that erstwhile life in the spirit realm and so fall victim to an Ahrimanically-oriented state of being.

That is the situation that has prevailed since the beginning of the fifteenth century. It was in preparation—for evolution is a gradual process—since the time of the Mystery of Golgotha, that greatest of earthly events designed to save man from the downfall to which he had necessarily to be exposed as a being destined for freedom.

It may be argued that man's share in what has taken place in this situation has been only semiconscious and that it has led to much good in the view of nature based on abstract ideas and in many a valid principle of conduct.

But this epoch, in which man was permitted to carry on his life unconsciously in Ahriman's dangerous domain, is now over.

Investigators of the spiritual world are obliged to call attention at this point in evolution to the spiritual fact of Michael's assumption of spiritual guidance in the affairs of men. Michael carries out what he is charged with accomplishing not by influencing man but rather leaving man free to follow him in order that human beings may, with Christ's help, again find their way out of that Ahrimanic realm into which they were required to enter.

Those who can feel themselves united with Anthroposophy in their innermost depths of soul will rightly understand this Michael mystery. Anthroposophy wants to be the messenger that brings word of this Michael mission.

*

GUIDELINES

1. Michael reascends the path that man followed in the course of his descent as he progressed through the successive stages of his spiritual development to arrive at the exercise of intelligence. But Michael will guide the will upward

18

on the path by which wisdom traveled downward on its way to its final stage, intelligence.

2. The fact that, from this point onward Michael *merely indicates* his path so that man may be left free to travel it, distinguishes this present Michael leadership from all earlier archangelic regencies and, indeed, from the earlier regencies of Michael himself. Those earlier regencies *worked actively* in human beings rather than merely showed *their* activity, and this made man of that time unable to be the free agent in his own activity.

3. Man's present task is to *understand* this, so that he will be able, whole-souled, to find his spiritual path in this new age of Michael.

V

MICHAEL'S EXPERIENCES IN THE FULFILLING
OF HIS COSMIC MISSION

Looking at things from the point of view of humanity, we can trace its progress from the level of consciousness on which man felt himself to be an integral part of the divine-spiritual order, to the present one on which he recognizes himself as an individual detached from that order and endowed with the power to think on his own. This was the way it was looked at in the previous issue of this Newsletter.

But it is also possible, in a supersensible approach, to project a picture of what Michael and his hosts experience during these developments; in other words, to look at them from Michael's standpoint. That attempt will now be made.

There was a first, most ancient period, of which one can only report what happened in the ranks of divine-spiritual beings and describe their ongoing activity. They bring to fulfillment what their inner natures prompt them to undertake, and they find satisfaction in doing it. What *they* experience in the process is the only thing to be considered. Such a thing as the human race is observable only in a remote corner of this divine activity, as one aspect of it.

The divine being, however, who, from the first, directed his attention to humanity, is Michael. He orders the gods' activity in such a way that man can have a place in that far corner of the cosmos. The way he carries on this course of action resembles what later developed in man as the manifestation of intellectual powers, the difference being that in Michael's case we have to do with a force actively streaming through the cosmos, structuring ideas and bringing reality to birth. In this force Michael is at work. It is his task to rule over cosmic intelligence. He wants to keep its further development in his

21

hands, something that can happen only if what works throughout the entire cosmos as intelligence eventually comes to be concentrated in the human individuality. The result is that a moment arrives in world evolution in which the cosmos no longer lives by its present, but by its past intelligence; the present intelligence is to be found in the stream of mankind's evolution.

Michael's desire is to keep what is thus developed as intelligence in the human race in continuing relationship with the divine-spiritual beings.

But something stands in the way of this achievement. What the gods undergo as their evolution in the course of separating intellectuality from their cosmic functioning in order to embody it in human nature is a cosmic fact open to observation. If beings exist with the requisite capacity to perceive this fact, they can make use of it for their own ends.— There are such beings: the Ahrimanic spirits. Such is their native endowment that they are able to absorb into themselves the intelligence detached from the gods, to incorporate into their own being the sum total of all intellectuality. This makes them the greatest, most comprehensive and penetrating intelligences in the universe.

Michael foresees how man, growing into an ever more independent use of intelligence, has to encounter the Ahrimanic beings and can become their victim in the ensuing relationship.—So Michael casts down the Ahrimanic forces, thrusting them constantly into a lower region than that in which man carries on his evolution. Michael, with the dragon under foot, casting him into the abyss; this is the mighty picture that lives in man's awareness of the above-described supersensible situation.

Evolution moves ahead. The intellectuality that began by being wholly encompassed by the realm of the divine spirit loosens its bond with that realm to the extent of becoming the ensouling element of the cosmos. What formerly merely rayed out from divine being now shines forth from the starry world as divine revelation. Where the world heretofore was guided by *divinity itself*, it is now guided by *divine revelation*, becomes objectified, behind which the godhead pursues the further course of *its own* evolution.

Again, Michael rules cosmic intelligence insofar as this flows, an ordered stream of ideas, through the manifestations of cosmic revelation.

The third phase of evolution brings a further detaching of cosmic intelligence from its origin. Henceforth, the present ordering of ideas no longer holds sway as divine revelation. The stars move in their orbits according to patterns of ideas embodied in them in the age just past. Michael perceives how the cosmic intellectuality over which he ruled in the universe becomes increasingly man's possession.

But Michael also sees the danger of man's falling victim to the Ahrimanic forces growing ever greater. He knows that as far as he is concerned, he can keep Ahriman underfoot. But can he achieve this for humanity as well?

Michael witnesses the occurrence of earth's greatest event. From the realm served by Michael, the Christ Being descends into the realm of earth in order to be present when intelligence has become fully the possession of individual man. That is the time when man experiences the strongest drive to give himself up to the power that has made itself the complete and perfect bearer of intellectuality. But the Christ will be there, living, by virtue of his great sacrifice, in the same sphere that Ahriman inhabits. Man will be able to choose between Christ and Ahriman. The world will be able to find the Christ-path in the course of mankind's evolution.

Such is Michael's cosmic experience with what he is given to rule over in the cosmos. In order to serve the trust with which he has been charged, he makes his way from the cosmos to the human scene. He has been traveling this path since the eighth century, but only in the last third of the nineteenth century did he enter upon the earthly office into which his cosmic office was transformed.

Michael has no power to compel human beings to anything. The fact that intelligence made its entrance into the domain of human individuality brought an end to compulsion. —But, in majestic exemplary deeds, Michael can carry out in the supersensible world bordering on the physical whatever he desires to do. He can reveal himself there in an aura of light and with a spiritual gesturing that brings to manifestation all the brilliance and glory of the past divine intelligence. He can show how the present-day effects of this intelligence of the past are truer, more beautiful, more teeming with virtue than anything that comes from Ahriman in the deceptive, seductive brilliance of today's intelligence. He can make evident the fact that *for him* Ahriman will always be the base spirit whom he treads underfoot.

Those individuals who behold the supersensible realm bordering on the visible world perceive Michael and his hosts there as described, carrying on their chosen work for humanity. Such individuals see how man is to be guided in freedom by the Michael-image through the Ahrimanic sphere, away from Ahriman and to the Christ. When such human beings succeed in opening the hearts and senses of their fellowmen by means of their vision, so that groups of human beings come to understand how Michael presently lives among them, mankind will begin to celebrate Michaelic festivals with the proper content, festivals that will enable souls to sense the Michael force living in them. Man will be *free* and yet he will pursue his spiritual path through the cosmos in inmost communion with the Christ.

*

GUIDELINES

1. To become rightly conscious of Michael's functioning in the spiritual world context means to separate the riddle of human freedom from its relationship to the cosmic background, insofar as this separation is necessary for earthly man.

2. For 'freedom' is an immediately given fact of innate experience of every human being who has become self-aware in the present period of human evolution. Nobody can say without denying an obvious fact that 'freedom does not exist.' But one might see a contradiction between what is thus actually given and cosmic processes. This contradiction disappears in contemplation of Michael's mission in the cosmos.

3. In my *Philosophy of Freedom*, human 'freedom' is shown to be a content of man's consciousness in the present epoch. The above picturing of the Michael mission shows how cosmically founded is the 'evolution' of this 'freedom.'

VI

THE HUMAN FUTURE AND MICHAEL'S ACTIVITY

How is man related to Michael and his hosts at the present stage of human evolution?

Man confronts a world that was once entirely divine-spiritual in nature, a world to which he belonged as an integral part of it. The world of his belonging was thus divine-spiritual. But at a subsequent evolutionary stage this was no longer the case; the world was a cosmic revelation of the divine-spiritual, its essential being hovering behind the revelation. But that being lived, nevertheless,and was active in the revelation. The starry world was already in existence, with the divine-spiritual living and active *as revelation* in its shining out and in its movement. It would be accurate to say that in the way a star stood or moved was a direct demonstration of the activity of the divine-spiritual.

Michael was as yet unopposed in his element in all the ways the divine spirit wrought in the cosmos and in the way man's life grew out of the cosmic activity of the divine-spiritual. Michael mediated the relationship of the divine to man.

Other times came. The starry world ceased to be a direct, immediate revelation of divine-spiritual activity. Rather did it live and move in continuation of such activity as had earlier been engendered in it. The divine-spiritual no longer lived in the cosmos as revelation, but only *as ongoing effect*. A definite split had appeared between divine-spiritual being and the universe; they were now separated. Michael remained with the divine-spiritual as his nature dictated, and sought to keep mankind also as close to it as possible. He continued to do this, for he wanted to shield man from living too strongly in a world that had become the mere *ongoing effect* of the divine-spiritual and was no longer either its essential being or its manifestation.

Michael counts it his deepest satisfaction that *through the agency of man* he has succeeded in keeping the starry world directly united with the divine-spiritual in the following way. When man has lived out his life between death and rebirth and is beginning his descent to a new earth existence, he *seeks*, on his way down, to establish harmony between the movements of the stars and his own life on earth. Unless man sought it, this harmony—which had previously been a matter of course because of the activity of the divine-spiritual in the stars, where human life also had its origin—would not presently exist in movements of the stars that had become the mere *effect* of previous activity. Man brings the divine-spiritual preserved in him from earlier times into relationship with the stars that contain the divine-spiritual only as an ongoing after-effect of those times. This brings a divine element into the relationship of man to world corresponding to that of earlier times, but which only *appears* in later ones. *It is Michael's deed* that this can be, and this deed causes him such deep satisfaction as to enable him to find in it part of his life-element, his life-energy, his sunlike life-will.

But when Michael turns his spiritual gaze today toward the earth he sees a basically different state of affairs. During man's life in the physical realm between birth and death, he is surrounded by a world that is, like himself, no longer subject to the direct working of the gods, but only to its after-effects, to what might be called *wrought-work*. This latter is of a wholly divine-spiritual nature in its forms; its divinity is manifest to man in those forms and in natural events, but is *no longer* a living presence in them. Nature is thus a God-wrought, divine creation, and everywhere an imaging forth of divine activity.

Man lives in this world of sun-like, but no longer living, divinity. As the result of Michael's work on him, however, he has preserved his human connection with divine-spiritual being. He lives as a God-permeated being in a non-God-permeated world.

Into this world emptied of God he will bring the content of *his* being as it has developed in the present epoch.

Humanity will take its increasing part in world evolution. The divine-spiritual element from which man sprang can, in the form of cosmically expanding human nature, illumine a cosmos now become merely the out-picturing of that divine spirit.

It is no longer the same being once present as the cosmos that will receive its illumination from humanity. As the divine-spiritual passes through humanness, it will experience a quality of being not previously manifested.

The hosts of Ahriman are up in arms against evolution taking this further course. They do not want the original divine-spiritual powers to illumine the universe in its further development; they want the cosmic intellectuality absorbed by them to irradiate the whole new cosmos-to-be and mankind to live its future life in this intellectualized and Ahriman-ized universe.

Man would forfeit the Christ in such a life. For Christ entered the world with the self-same intellectuality that lived in the divine-spiritual when its *essential being* was still engaged in creating the cosmos. If what we say today is based on thoughts such as the Christ would have, we counter the Ahrimanic powers with an element that keeps us from falling victim to them.

We can speak in this way if we grasp the meaning of Michael's cosmic mission. We have to learn to speak about nature today in a way that satisfies the requirements of the consciousness soul level of development. Though we have to imbue ourselves with the purely scientific mode of thinking, we should nevertheless learn to speak of—that is, to *feel* —*nature* in a way consonant with the Christ. We should

learn the Christ way of speaking not only when we are talk-
ing of becoming free of nature or discussing soul and spiritual matters, but in reference to the cosmic world as well.

If, with heartfelt inner sensing, we live wholly into what
Michael and his hosts are doing in their mission among us,
we will preserve our human connection with the divine-
spiritual and come to understand how to nurture the language of Christ when we are speaking about cosmic matters.

For to understand Michael means today to find the way to
the Logos, which Christ lives among men on earth.

Anthroposophy truly values what the scientific mode of
thinking of the past four or five centuries has learned to
report about the universe. But it also speaks in another way
about man's being, about his evolution, and about cosmic
development. Its desire is to speak the language of Christ
and Michael.

If both languages are spoken, there will be no break in the
continuity of development; it cannot then succumb to Ahriman and fail to find its way back to the original divine spirit.
The merely natural scientific way of speaking corresponds to
the detachment of intellectuality from its divine-spiritual
origin. It *can* trend into the Ahrimanic if no attention is paid
to Michael's mission. But it *will not* do so if the newly freed
intellect, strengthened by Michael's example, again finds
itself in the original cosmic intellectuality now detached from
man and become objective to him—the intellectuality of
man's beginning, which appeared in the living Christ within
the human domain after it had withdrawn from man for his
freedom's sake.

*

GUIDELINES

1. The divine-spiritual manifests itself in the cosmos in
the following phases in a variety of ways: In its own primal,
essential *being*; in the *revelation* of that being; in *ongoing ef-*

fects after that being withdrew from revelation; in the *wrought-work* observable in the created universe, when only the forms of its creation remained.

2. In contemporary man's view of nature he is no longer related to the divine, but only to its works. In itself, this view can just as well unite him humanly with the Christ forces as with those of Ahriman.

3. Michael is imbued with the striving to embody in cosmic-human evolution, by means of his non-compelling example, the relationship of man to the cosmos preserved from the time when essential divine being and its revelation were still in evidence, so that the view of nature based on the out-picturing, the empty form of the divine may progress to a higher, spiritual view of nature's world. This view will indeed be entertained by man, but simply as an after-image of divinity's relationship to the cosmos during the first two phases of cosmic development. Herein, Anthroposophy supports the view of nature inherent in the consciousness-soul age, but supplements it with another view that derives from looking at things with the eyes of the spirit.

VII

MAN'S MICHAEL-CHRIST EXPERIENCE

A person who gives himself in a truly heartfelt way to inner contemplation of Michael's deeds and being will come to a real understanding of the way man has to conceive a world that is no longer either divine being or its revelation, nor yet ongoing effect, but simply the gods' wrought-work. To look into this world with insight is to have shapes and forms in view that everywhere speak plainly of divinity, but in which self-sustaining divine being is no longer to be found unless one gives oneself up to illusion. One should not restrict one's insight to the merely knowable. The configuration of the world surrounding man today manifests itself most clearly to this view. But of far greater import for everyday life is the feeling, the will, the working in a world felt to be formed, indeed, in accordance with the divine image but not to be experienced as God-enlivened. To bring genuine moral life into a world of this kind requires the generating of ethical impulses such as are described in my *Philosophy of Freedom.*

Michael's being and present sphere of action can shine out in this wrought-work world for those of true feeling. Michael does not make an appearance in the physical realm; he restricts himself and all his activity to a supersensible region immediately bordering on the physical world as this exists in the present phase of cosmic evolution. This renders it impossible that the impression of Michael's being received by humans could mislead them into a fantastic view of nature, or make them try to share cultural-practical life in their God-wrought but not God-enlivened world as though they could be impelled to action by any but their own ethical-spiritual impulses. Whether thinking or willing, man will always have to approach Michael by transposing himself into the spiritual realms.

In so doing, man will live spiritually in the following way. He will take knowledge and life as they have had to be taken since the fifteenth century. But he will hold fast to the Michaelic revelation, letting it shine like a light illumining his thoughts as he garners them from the world of nature; he will carry them in his heart as warmth, even though he must live in accordance with the world of divine wrought-works. He will not only observe and experience the present-day world, but also that world mediated by Michael as well—a *past* state of the world, one brought by Michael's deeds and being into the present.

If it were otherwise, if Michael's activity were such that he brought his deeds into the world that man has to know and experience as physical, then man would presently be experiencing something of the world that really *was* once upon a time, but that *is* no longer. If such a thing were to come to pass, this illusory grasp of the world would lead man's soul away from reality suited to it and into another, a Luciferic sphere.

Michael's way of making the past effective in man's present experience is in keeping with the purposes of true spiritual world progress, in which nothing of a Luciferic nature has a part. It is important for human souls, in their conceiving of Michael's mission, to have a right picture of its avoidance of everything Luciferic.

This understanding of the Michaelic-light making its appearance on the scene of human history provides the basis for finding the right approach to Christ as well.

Michael provides the proper orientation in those concerns where man approaches the world around him in knowledge and action, whereas he will have to find an inner path to Christ.

Considering the form that our approach to nature has assumed during the last five centuries, it is thoroughly understandable that supersensible knowledge, too, should have become what it is today in modern man's conceiving.

Nature has to be known and experienced as devoid of God. But, in this kind of relationship to the world, man is no longer able to experience himself. The relationship to nature that comes naturally to him as a self in this epoch gives him *no* understanding of himself as a supersensible being, and with only this relationship in view, he cannot live ethically in a way attuned to his humanity.

So it has come about that this way of living and experiencing is not allowed to come into contact with anything that has to do with man's supersensible being, or, indeed, with the supersensible world. That realm is considered inaccessible to human knowing. An extra- or super-scientific realm of belief and revelation has to be postulated in addition to the scientifically knowable.

But the purely spiritual activity of Christ presents the opposite picture. Ever since the Mystery of Golgotha, it has been possible to reach Him. The relationship to Him need not remain a vague, mystical one of unillumined feeling; it can become a fully concrete, deep, clear human experience.

From this communion with the Christ the human soul garners what it needs to know about its own supersensible nature. The revelation of faith must be felt to receive a constant influx of living experience of the Christ. To feel Him to be the Being who mediates to the human soul the perception of its own supersensible nature leads to life's thorough Christianizing.

The Michael experience and the Christ experience can thus stand side by side. Michael will guide man in the right way to a supersensible experience of nature, and the outlook on nature will be able to take its place, undistorted, alongside a spiritual view of the world and of man as a universal being.

Through a right relationship to Christ, man will experience in living soul-intercourse with Him what he could otherwise receive only in the form of traditional revelations of faith. The inner world of the soul's experience can then be experienced as spiritually illumined, the outer world of nature as spiritually sustained.

If man were to try to attain insight into his own supersensible being without communion with the Christ, he would be seduced away from himself and into the realm of Ahriman. Christ is the cosmically ordained carrier of humanity's impulses toward the future. For the human soul to unite with Him means receiving into itself, for cosmically intended nurturing, the seeds of its own future. Other beings whose present-day forms are such as the cosmos intends for man only in the future belong to the Ahrimanic sphere. Union with the Christ means protecting oneself properly from Ahrimanic influences.

Those individuals who insist on keeping traditional religious revelation free of any inclusion of human knowledge betray the fear that man may otherwise fall victim to Ahrimanic influences. We have to understand this fear. But it is necessary, on the other hand, to understand how it contributes to the honoring and acknowledging of Christ when the experience of Him is ascribed to the grace-filled flowing of the spiritual into human souls.

Thus the Michael experience and the Christ experience can stand side by side in future. This will enable man to travel his true path of freedom between seduction by Luciferic illusions in his thinking and living, and Ahrimanic enticement into a future shape of things that satisfy his conceit but does not rightly belong to *him* in the present epoch.

To fall victim to Luciferic illusions means to fall short of becoming fully human; that is, to fail to make the effort to progress to the stage of freedom, remaining content to stay at the earlier evolutionary God-man level. To fall victim to Ahrimanic enticement means being unwilling to wait for the right cosmic moment to come to a certain stage of human-ness and instead to take this stage prematurely.

In future, Michael-Christ will stand as path-indicators at the start of the route along which man, in keeping with cosmic goals, can advance between Lucifer and Ahriman and arrive at his world destination.

*

GUIDELINES

1. Man travels his path through the cosmos in a way that allows Lucifer to distort his view into the past, and Ahriman his sensing of the future.

2. Man finds the right relationship to Lucifer's distortions by imbuing his attitude toward life and knowledge with a sense of Michael's being and mission.

3. He thereby safeguards himself against the enticements of Ahriman as well, for the spiritual path by which Michael directs man into external nature leads to the proper relation-ship with Ahriman in that it brings man to a true Christ experience.

VIII

MICHAEL'S MISSION
IN THE COSMIC AGE OF HUMAN FREEDOM

If one approaches the study of Michael's contemporary mission, experiencing it spiritually, it becomes possible to see the cosmic nature of freedom in spiritual-scientific illumination.

This is not meant with reference to my *Philosophy of Freedom*, a work based on purely human cognitive powers, when they can be applied to the realm of the spirit. One does not need to commune with beings of other worlds to attain the kind of insight dealt with there. But it might be said that the *Philosophy of Freedom* prepares the reader for an understanding of freedom that can become actual experience of spiritual communion with Michael.

That experience may be described as follows.

If freedom is really to underlie human action, what is done in its light may not depend in any way whatsoever on man's physical and etheric organization. Free deeds can issue only from the ego, and the astral body must be able to attune itself to this free ego activity in order to transmit it to the physical and etheric bodies. But this is only one aspect of the matter; the other becomes clear when we relate it to Michael's mission. —What human beings experience in freedom may also not be allowed to influence their physical and etheric bodies in any way. If that were to happen, man would lose all connection with what he has become in his passage through the stages of his development influenced by divine-spiritual *being* and divine-spiritual *revelation*.

Man's experience of what remains the *mere wrought-work of his divine-spiritual surroundings* must not exert an influence on anything but the spirit (or ego) element in him. The only thing permitted to influence his physical and etheric

39

organism is what began within the being and revelation of the divine-spiritual and continues on within man's own being, not what lies outside him. This must not come in touch in human nature with what lives within it as the freedom element.

That this is possible derives solely from the fact that Michael carries over from a primeval period of evolution something that connects man with divine-spiritual reality without exercising any present effect on his physical and etheric structure. This provides the basis in Michael's mission for human communion with the spiritual world that takes place without involving natural processes.

It is elevating to witness how Michael lifts man's being into the sphere of the spirit while his unconscious or subconscious aspects, developing below the level where freedom reigns, grow ever more deeply involved with matter.

Man's position in relationship to the being of the world will become an increasing puzzle to him if he does not rise to recognition of such matters as Michael's mission while still feeling his ties with nature's beings and processes.—The ties with nature are learned as though from external perception; those with the spiritual world issue from something resembling an inner conversation with a form of being to which one gains access by opening oneself to a spiritual view of the universe.

In order for man to carry out impulses conceived in freedom, he must be able to keep certain workings of nature that act upon his being from out of the cosmos from affecting him. This keeping at arm's length goes on in the subconsciousness when there are active in him, on the conscious level, forces that support the life of the ego in freedom. Awareness of free action is a matter of inward perception for man himself; but for spiritual beings, who relate to man from other spheres of the world, the situation is a different one. The being from the hierarchy of angels who is charged with carrying over man's existence from one earthly life to another is at once aware, in witnessing free human action, that the human being involved is repelling cosmic forces that seek to go on shaping him, forces that are trying to continue giving his ego organization such necessary physical support as they gave it before the Age of Michael set in.

As a being of archangelic rank, Michael receives his impressions with the help of beings of the rank of angels. He devotes himself, in the way described, to the task of conveying to man, from out of the spiritual realms of the cosmos, forces that can act as a replacement for suppressed natural forces.

He achieves this by bringing his activity into the most perfect attunement with the Mystery of Golgotha.

Christ's activity in earth evolution harbors the forces needed by man, when he acts in freedom, to balance out the suppressed impulses that derive from nature. But he must then devote his soul truly to that inner communion with the Christ that was spoken of in these communications on the subject of the Michael mission.

Human beings are aware that they are confronting reality when they confront the physical sun and are recipients of its light and warmth. Just so must they live in relationship to Christ, the spiritual sun, which has united its existence with that of earth, and take up livingly into their souls what corresponds in the spiritual world to warmth and light.

They will feel themselves permeated by 'spiritual warmth' as they experience 'Christ within them,' and will say as they sense this permeation: "This warmth frees my humanity from cosmic ties by which it must not remain bound. The divine-spiritual existence of primeval times had the task of bringing me to the attainment of freedom in regions in which it cannot accompany me further, but in which it gave me the Christ in order that His forces endow me as a free man with what was once supplied by the divine-spiritual existence of primeval times as a natural endowment; at that time, how-

41

ever, the way of nature and the way of the spirit were one. This warmth restores me once again to the divine element from which I sprang."

As they feel this, men's experience in and with the Christ will become one in innermost soul-warmth with the experience of true, genuine humanness. "Christ gives me my human nature." Such will be the profound sense suffusing the soul to its depths. And after one has experienced this feeling, one goes on further to one in which the individual senses himself raised up by the Christ beyond mere earthly existence, becoming one with the starry surroundings that encompass the earth and with everything divine-spiritual to be met with there.

The same holds true of spiritual light. An individual can sense his humanity in fullness when he becomes aware of himself as a free agent. But a certain darkness accompanies this experience. The ancient divine-spiritual source of light no longer shines. But the light with which Christ endows man's ego restores that primeval illumination. In communion of this kind with the Christ, man's whole soul can be irradiated by the sun-like thought: "The glorious divine light of ancient days lives again and shines out, though its luminosity is not that of nature." Man unites himself in the present with the spiritual-cosmic light forces from a distant past in which he was not as yet a free individuality. If he understands and unites his soul with the Michael mission, he can find in this illumination his guide for traveling his rightful human path.

This means that he will feel in spiritual warmth the impulse that will carry him into his cosmic future in a way that enables him to remain true to the original gifts given him by divine-spiritual beings even though he has evolved in their realm to the stage of free individuality. He will sense in spiritual light the force that will lead him, with an ever higher and more inclusive perceptive consciousness, to the world in which he finds himself together again, as a free agent with the gods of his origin.

If he were to shy away from a full experience of freedom and become fixed in his original state of existence, willing to continue on in the condition of primeval, naive divine grace that once prevailed, he would be led to Lucifer, whose desire it is to reject the world as it is today.

If he were to accept the present state of things, content to let only that universal rule of natural law conceived by a morally neutral intellect prevail while restricting himself to a merely mental experience of freedom, he would be led—in this age, when evolution must be continued into deeper regions of the soul to counterbalance those higher ones in which freedom reigns—to Ahriman, who would like to see the contemporary world turned into a purely intellectual cosmos.

These are the regions where security and certainty flourish in the souls and spirits of human beings who see Michael in spirit as they look outward and the Christ as they look inward —a certainty and security that make it possible for them to travel the cosmic path on which, without losing touch with their origin, they will find their rightful future perfecting.

*

GUIDELINES

1. A free act can only be one in which natural processes play no part in man, either from within or without.

2. The polar opposite of a situation in which these natural processes are suppressed in the free deeds of human individuals would be an action made unfree by the presence of these processes, and would give man his cosmically predetermined form.

3. This form, which an individual whose being is attuned to present and future stages of cosmic evolution does *not* naturally assume, comes to him *spiritually* when he unites himself with Michael, and through this union finds his way to Christ as well.

.

IX

COSMIC THOUGHTS IN THE ACTIVITY OF MICHAEL
AND IN THE ACTIVITY OF AHRIMAN

A person studying the relationship of Michael to Ahriman is impelled to question how these two spiritual forces relate to one another from a cosmic aspect, since both are actively engaged in the development of intellectual capacities.

Michael was the being who, in the past, developed intellectuality throughout the cosmos. He performed this function as the servant of those divine-spiritual powers from which both he and the human race issued, and he desires to remain constant in this relationship to intellectuality. When intellect broke away from the divine-spiritual to make its way into man's inner being, Michael made the decision to enter into such a relationship with mankind as to find therein a continuing relationship to the intellectual element. But he wanted to do this wholly in harmony with the aims of those divine-spiritual beings whose servant he is and with whom he, like the human race, has been connected from the time of his origin. So he intends to see that intellectuality takes its future course through the hearts of human beings, remaining always the same force it was when, in the beginning, it flowed out of the inwardness of divine-spiritual beings.

In Ahriman's case an entirely different situation prevails. This being long ago disassociated himself from the mainstream of evolution to which the aforementioned divine-spiritual powers belong, having in the far past set himself up alongside them as an independent cosmic force. —Although Ahriman presently exists in the same world that man inhabits, he undertakes no joint effort with the beings who rightfully belong there. It is only because the intellectuality detached from divine-spiritual beings is making its way into this world that Ahriman in his relationship to intellectuality can use it as a means of connecting himself with the human race. For he united himself in a far distant past with what man is presently receiving as a gift from the cosmos. If Ahriman achieves his aim, he would make the intellect man thus receives similar to his own. —

Now Ahriman acquired intellectuality at a time when he could not make it an inner capacity. So it remained in his case an energy lacking any heart and soul involvement, flowing out of him as an ice-cold, soulless cosmic impulse. Those human beings who succumb to it develop a merciless, loveless logic, which, although it seems to speak objectively, really issues from Ahriman. It is devoid of any true, heartfelt soul connection with what the person in question is thinking, saying or doing.

Michael, on the other hand, never acquired intellectuality as his own attribute. He administers it as a divine-spiritual force, feeling himself at one with divine-spiritual powers. His wielding of intellectuality makes it every bit as much an attribute of heart and soul as it is of head and mind, for Michael is the bearer of all the primeval forces issuing from his gods and from man's origin. So he imparts to intellectuality nothing of a frigidly cold, soulless quality, but he is related to it with heartfelt warmth of soul.

This is also the reason why Michael pursues his course through the cosmos with characteristically grave mien and gesture. To be thus inwardly connected with the content of intelligence means having to meet the challenge of avoiding the injection of any subjective or arbitrary element of wish or self-will into that content. Otherwise, logic would be synonymous with the self-will of one being rather than the expression of the cosmos. Michael regards it as *his* forte to keep his being strictly the expression of cosmic being; whatever stirs within him must remain within. His attention is to the great concerns of the cosmos, and his mien reflects this. In approaching human beings, his will must mirror what he has perceived in the cosmos; his bearing and gesture convey this. Michael is in all respects *grave*, for gravity in a being's bearing is a mirroring of the cosmos in that being; while to smile expresses rather what radiates from within a being into the world about.

One imagination of Michael is the following. He reigns through *the course of time* clad in cosmic light as his essential being, shaping cosmic warmth as the revelation of his nature. As a *being*, he conducts himself *like a world*, asserts himself only as he asserts the world, guiding forces earthward from every corner of the universe.

Ahriman's is the opposite imagination. He would like to wrest *time from space* in his course. He sends rays of his own light into the darkness that surrounds him. The more he brings his aims to fulfillment, the frostier grows his environment. He moves like a world completely compressed into a single being, that of himself alone, asserting himself while denying the world. His movement suggests uncanny forces issuing from dark earth caverns to cling about him.

When an individual seeks freedom with no tendency to egoism, when freedom becomes for him pure love of the action he is carrying out, then he finds it possible to approach Michael. But if he attempts free actions while tainted with egoistic striving, if his freedom means a *proud* exhibiting of *himself* in his deeds, he is in danger of straying into Ahriman's realm.

The imaginations here described flash up as the product either of an individual's love of the deed he performs (Michael) or of the self-love that motivates his action (Ahriman).

When a person feels himself as a free being close to Michael, he is moving toward a permeation of his whole human selfhood with the power of intellectuality. Although he thinks with his head, his heart feels the light or darkness of his thought. His will rays forth his humanity when he senses his thoughts moving in him as intentions. As he becomes an expression of the world, he becomes ever more

47

fully human; he finds himself not through *self-seeking* but through a love-imbued will-relationship to the world.

When a person becomes a victim of ahrimanic seduction as he develops freedom, he is enticed into an intellectuality like a spiritual automatism in which he is no longer himself but just part of a mechanism. All his thinking is then mere head experience; this cuts it off from being an experience of his own heart and will life and obscures his sense of individuality. He loses more and more of the inner imprint of humanness that makes one an individual. He loses himself in self-seeking. He withdraws from a world to which he refuses to give his love, but it is only through loving the world that he can develop the experience of selfhood.

The above considerations make it understandable that Michael is the guide to Christ. Michael goes his loving way through the world with the full gravity of his nature, his bearing, his action. Those who adhere to him *act lovingly in relation to the world about them.* For love must flow out to the surrounding world; otherwise it becomes self-love.

If this love is present in one's Michael orientation, *love for others* can radiate back into one's own self, which finds it possible to love without self-love. Human souls find the Christ as they take this path.

Those who adhere to Michael *radiate love* toward the world around them and are thereby enabled to develop the relationship to the inner world of their souls that guides them to a meeting with the Christ.

The age just beginning is in need of human awareness of that world immediately bordering on the realm we know as the physical—a world wherein the being and mission of Michael described above are to be experienced. For the realm pictured as the natural world by human beings whose attention is focused on the physical is not the world in which they actually live, but rather one as far *beneath* the truly human sphere as the Michaelic world is elevated *above* it. We simply do not notice that, as we form a picture of our world, another world-picture comes into being in our consciousness , involving us in a process of eliminating ourselves and falling prey to spiritual automatism. We can preserve our humanity only by countering *this* picture—which, in its focus on nature, threatens us with a loss of self—with that other in which Michael reigns and points the way to Christ.

*

GUIDELINES

1. We do not truly grasp what significance an active force such as world-thoughts has for the world if we consider it only from the standpoint of the activity itself. We need instead to come to an understanding of the beings from whom the activity issues. In the case of world-thoughts, this means discriminating between Michael and Ahriman as beings who bring thoughts into the world and transmit them.

2. What, in the one case, can be beneficial and creative because of the nature of the relationship to the world of the being involved, can prove ruinous and destructive when it issues from the other. When man receives world-thoughts from Michael, they carry him into the future, whereas they lead him astray from a wholesome future course if Ahriman succeeds in transmitting them.

3. Through contemplation of matters such as these one is helped to overcome more and more that vague spirituality that sees an underlying pantheistic causation at work behind everything; it guides us to a clear, concrete grasp that is able to form concepts of the *divine beings* of the higher hierarchies. For all reality is at bottom a matter of the beings involved, and whatever is not actual being is the activity that takes place in the relationships between beings. This activity can be understood only by those able to penetrate to the beings that engender it.

X

FIRST CONTEMPLATION:
AT THE THRESHOLD OF THE CONSCIOUSNESS SOUL
HOW MICHAEL PREPARES HIS EARTHLY MISSION
SUPERSENSIBLY BY OVERCOMING LUCIFER

Michael's intervention in the evolution of the world and man at the end of the nineteenth century appears in a special light when we contemplate the spiritual history of the preceding centuries.

The consciousness-soul epoch began at the outset of the fifteenth century. A complete transformation of mankind's spiritual life took place prior to this time. There is evidence that, heretofore, imaginations commonly influenced the way people looked at things. Although it is true that there were individuals here and there who had already progressed to the point of entertaining mere concepts in their soul lives, the prevailing state of the majority of human beings was one in which imaginations intermingled with mental pictures derived from the purely physical scene. That holds true both in the case of concepts of nature and of historical events.

External evidence confirms what spiritual observation has discovered in this respect. A few examples can be cited.

Accounts showing how historical events were regarded and spoken of in the preceding centuries were written down just before the dawning of the consciousness-soul age. This has meant that *sagas* and other such tales of that period were preserved and have come down to us, providing a faithful picturing of that earlier conceiving of "history."

A beautiful example is the story of "The Good Gerhard," contained in a poem by Rudolf von Ems, who lived in the first part of the thirteenth century. "Good Gerhard" is a rich merchant of Cologne. He undertakes a trading expedition to Russia, Lithuania and Prussia to buy sables. He then continues onward to Damascus and Nineveh to procure silks and other such merchandise.

On the homeward journey, he is driven off course by a storm. Arriving in an unfamiliar country, he makes the acquaintance of a man who has made prisoners of some English knights and the betrothed bride of the king of England. Gerhard exchanges all the proceeds of his trading expedition for the captives, whom he takes aboard his ship. He sets sail on the homeward voyage. When the ships reach the port where Gerhard's route to his homeland and that of the English knights separate, he frees the knights to return to England, but keeps the promised bride of England's king with him in the hope that King William will come to fetch her as soon as he hears of her release and learns of her whereabouts. Gerhard treats her and her retinue with every courtesy; she lives like a cherished daughter in the house of her rescuer.

A long span of time passes with no sign of the king's coming to fetch her. Since it seems possible that William may be dead, Gerhard decides to wed her to his son to secure her future. In the midst of the wedding ceremonies, William makes his appearance in the guise of a pilgrim. He has been wandering about on a long search for his lost bride. Gerhard's son unselfishly restores her to King William. She and the king remain a while at Gerhard's home; then William outfits a ship for their return to England.

The erstwhile prisoners whom Gerhard had freed from captivity have meanwhile recovered all their former position and prestige in England. When Gerhard visits their country, they hail him as the man they want for king. He replies that he has brought back their rightful rulers. They, too, had believed William dead, and wished to appoint a new ruler, so chaotic had conditions become during the king's long absence. Gerhard refuses all the honors and rewards offered him and returns to Cologne, where he becomes once again the simple merchant he had always been.

The story adds a further detail. The Saxon emperor, Otto the First, travels to Cologne to make the acquaintance of "The Good Gerhard." This mighty ruler had succumbed to the temptation of expecting "earthly rewards" for much that he had accomplished. He learns from knowing Gerhard what great good a simple man can do: The sacrifice of all his wares to free captives, restoring his son's bride to William, going to the great trouble involved in transporting the king back to England, and so on—all this without any desire for earthly rewards, looking for compensation to God alone. Everyone calls this man "the Good Gerhard," and the emperor undergoes a great moral-religious awakening as a result of his exposure to Gerhard's attitude.

The story I have told in outline here, since it is not sufficiently well-known to be recognized by its title alone, reveals clearly *from one aspect* what the state of soul was in the period prior to the advent of the consciousness soul in mankind's evolution.

Anyone who lets the story told by Rudolf von Ems work upon him can sense what a change has come about in the way the earthly world is experienced since the time of Emperor Otto's reign in the tenth century.

Notice how sharply bright the world has become in man's perceiving of physical facts and processes in the consciousness soul period. Gerhard and his ships travel as though in a fog. He knows only small fragments of the world with which he seeks some connection. People in Cologne know nothing of what is going on in England, and a person has to search for years for someone in Cologne. The life and belongings of a person like the man on whose shore Gerhard was cast up are known only to one whose destiny brings him to that very spot. Awareness of today's world situation seems, in contrast to that of Gerhard's time, like looking out over a vast, sunlit landscape compared to feeling one's way through a dense mist.

The story of "Good Gerhard" has no sort of relevance to what is accepted as valid "history" in our time. All the more, however, does it exemplify the feeling and the whole spiritual situation of that period. These, rather than single physical events, are pictured in imaginations.

The story reflects how a man of that time felt himself to be not just a person living and acting as a link in the chain of events occurring on the physical plane, but as one into whose life on earth spiritual, supersensible beings projected their activity, as one whose will was bound up with theirs.

The story of "Good Gerhard" shows how the twilight dimness that obscured the physical universe to men's penetration prior to the age of the consciousness soul caused their gaze to be directed toward the spiritual world. Their incapacity to experience the *extension* of the physical world made people all the more able to experience the *depths* of the spiritual.

But the dim, dreamlike clairvoyance that had enabled men of old to behold the spiritual world, no longer prevailed in the period we have been considering. Imaginations were still present, but they arose in human souls already strongly impulsed in a thought-direction. This resulted in an incapacity properly to relate the world revealed by imaginations to the world of physical experience. People whose allegiance was more to the life of thinking therefore tended to look upon imaginations as 'fabrications' lacking any relationship to reality.

People no longer realized that imaginations provided glimpses of a world experienced with an entirely different part of their human entelechy than that with which the physical world is experienced. Accounts therefore presented both worlds side by side. In the way stories were told, both were so presented that it was possible to conceive the spiritual events described as having taken place just as perceptibly as the physical events recounted.

Not only was this the case, but we must also reckon with the fact that in many such accounts physical events are jumbled together. Individuals who lived in different centuries are spoken of as contemporaries. Events are laid in the wrong locale or attributed to incorrect periods.

Human souls looked at facts in a way suited only to spiritual matters where time and space have a different relevance. The physical world is presented in imaginations instead of in thoughts and, on the other hand, the spiritual world is introduced into the story as though one were dealing not with an entirely different form of existence but with the continuation of events on the physical plane.

The concept of history that limits itself to physical events holds that the old-time imaginations of the Orient, of Greece, and so on, were simply carried over and incorporated into historical matters of concern to those early times. In the seventh century writings of Isidore of Seville, for example, one is dealing with just such a collection of old legendary 'motifs.'

But this is an external view of things that can have meaning only for people without any feeling for *the* state of soul of human beings still aware that their lives were directly linked to the world of the spirit and who felt impelled to give this expression in imaginative form. If, instead of a personal imagination, a historically transmitted one with which one has become familiar is resorted to, that is immaterial. What matters is that the soul is oriented to the spiritual world in a way that views both its own activity and natural events as interwoven with that world.

Nevertheless, the story-telling style of the period prior to the dawning of the consciousness-soul age does show confusion and spiritual observation sees in this confusion the effects of Luciferic activity.

The impulse souls felt to drink in imaginations as part of their content of experience is due not so much to the capacities with which their dreamlike clairvoyance endowed them in those early times as it is to other faculties that they possessed from the eighth to the fourteenth centuries. *These* capacities lay more in the direction of a thinking approach to what their senses perceived. Both types of capacities existed side by side in that transitional period. Souls occupied a vantage point *between* the old orientation toward the spiritual world that perceived physical things only as though in a mist, and the new outlook that was concerned with physical occurrences and possessed a lessening power of spiritual vision.

Luciferic forces were active in this situation of unstable balance. They wanted to keep man from becoming completely oriented to the physical world. Their desire was, and is, to restrict his consciousness to those regions of the spirit suited to his primeval state of being, preventing pure thoughts directed toward a grasp of physical existence from flowing into his dreamlike, imaginative world perception. They can exercise an improper restraint on his capacity to perceive the physical world, but are nevertheless unable properly to maintain his erstwhile imaginative experience, with the result that, though he may be prone to imaginative musing, they cannot transport him into the realm where imaginations have full validity.

At the dawning of the consciousness-soul age, Lucifer's influence is such that man is transposed into the supersensible realm that borders on the physical. This is evident in the "Legend of Duke Ernest," one of the favorite stories of the Middle Ages, known far and wide.

Duke Ernest comes into conflict with the Emperor, who goes to war against him in an unjust effort to destroy him. Duke Ernest feels compelled to flee from this impossible relationship with the ruler by joining the crusade then traveling to the East. His experiences en route exemplify what has been stated about the "legendary" interweaving of physical and spiritual elements. He comes, for example, upon a race of people with heads like those of cranes. He and his ships are wrecked on the shores of a "magnetic mountain" that attracts them to it so that no one who approaches it can get away and must die a miserable death. Duke Ernest and his followers escape by sewing themselves into skins and letting griffins, accustomed to preying upon people shipwrecked upon the magnetic mountain, carry them away to a mountain top, where, in the griffins' absence, they cut themselves out of the skins and escape. Further wanderings bring them to a people whose ears are so long that they can wrap them around their entire bodies, and to another folk with feet so large that when it rains they can lie on the ground and hold their feet above them like umbrellas. They come to a race of dwarves, of giants, and so on. Many such adventures are recounted as befalling Duke Ernest on his crusading journey. The "saga" fails to convey a true impression of the way the story is oriented to the spiritual realm wherever imaginations enter in, of the way pictures are used to describe things that happen in the astral world and are connected with the will and destiny of earthlings.

This is true, too, of the beautiful story of Roland, which celebrates Charlemagne's Spanish campaign against the heathens. Like the Bible, it even states that the sun slows its course to make one day last as long as two so that Charlemagne can arrive at a place he is intent upon reaching.

We see, too, how the form of the *Nibelungen Saga* handed down in more northerly countries lays more stress on visions of the spiritual, in contrast to the way the Middle European version brings imaginations closer to life on the physical plane. The northern form clearly states that the imaginations refer to an 'astral' world, whereas in that of Middle Europe imaginations slide over into a picturing of the physical.

Imaginations appearing in the legend of Duke Ernest also really refer to experiences that, *alternating* with those on the physical plane, take place in an 'astral' world to which man belongs every bit as much as he does to the physical.

When we look at all this from a spiritual standpoint, we see how entering upon the consciousness-soul age meant growing out of an evolutionary phase that would have brought about man's overpowering by the Luciferic forces had not the consciousness soul, with its intellectual capacity, introduced a new evolutionary impulse into human nature. The consciousness soul prevented an orientation toward the spiritual world that threatened to lead mankind astray; the attention of human beings was attracted outward, to a concern with the physical universe. Everything that took place in this direction had the effect of helping humanity escape the confusion created by the Luciferic powers.

In all this, Michael was already active on man's behalf from out of the realm of the spirit, preparing supersensibly for his coming task. He endowed the human race with impulses that preserved its primeval relationship to the divine-spiritual world without running the danger of that preservation assuming a Luciferic character.

Then, in the final third of the nineteenth century, Michael penetrated into the physical world itself with the activity he had been carrying on, in a preparatory way in the spiritual realm, from the fifteenth to the nineteenth centuries.

For a certain period of time, humanity's spiritual evolution had to be aimed at freeing man from a relationship to the spiritual world that threatened to become unsuitable. When that was accomplished, Michael's mission guided this evolution onto paths whereby man's progressive continuance on earth was once again brought into a wholesome relationship to the spiritual world.

Michael may thus be seen standing with his activity midway between a Luciferic *world picture* and an Ahrimanic *world intellect*. The former is forged by Michael into a wisdom permeated *world revelation*, which shows us world intellect as divine *world activity*. In this *world activity*, which can thus disclose itself to human hearts as the product of Michael's world revelation, lives Christ's caring for the human race.

*

GUIDELINES

1. The dawning of the consciousness-soul age in the fifteenth century was preceded in the twilight dimming of the

age of the intellectual soul by an intensifying activity on the part of Lucifer. This continues for a while into the new epoch.

2. This Luciferic activity had as its goal the untimely preservation of old forms of conceiving the world, thus preventing man from progressing to an intellectual grasp of the physical life of the universe and from taking part in it.

3. Michael joins forces with man's activity in order to keep independent intellectuality related to the divine-spiritual source of its origin, but this in a rightful rather than in a Luciferic way.

XI

SECOND CONTEMPLATION:
HOW THE MICHAEL FORCES WORK ON THE
EARLY DEVELOPMENT OF THE CONSCIOUSNESS SOUL

In the period during which the consciousness soul was making its entry into man's earthly evolution, it was difficult for the beings of the spiritual realm closest to earthly life to approach humanity. Earthly events take on a form indicating that quite special conditions are required to give the spiritual access to the physical life of man. But, on the other hand, this form also indicates, often in an exceedingly illuminating way, how one spiritual element, actively opposing another, seeks to enter into human earthly life when the forces of the past are *still* at work and those of the future are already *beginning* to act.

A war, lasting over a century (1339-1453), broke out between France and England and brought about confusing conditions. In this confusion, which was the product of a spiritual stream unfavorable to human development, events that should have taken place to bring the consciousness soul more swiftly into human experience were prevented from occurring as they otherwise would have. Chaucer, who died in 1400, was the founder of English literature. We need only consider the spiritual consequences for Europe that grew out of the founding of this literature to see significance in the fact that this event could not shape itself in an undisturbed atmosphere, but occurred instead in wartime confusion. There is the further fact that, before this happened, England witnessed the birth in 1215 of that political thinking that can derive its proper character from the consciousness soul. The further developments of this event were also subject to war-created hindrances.

We are witnessing here a period in which the spiritual forces desirous of developing man further in accordance with the design laid down in him from the beginning by still loftier powers come up against opposition. These opponents want to deflect man into other than his primordially appointed paths. If that were to happen, he would be unable to use the forces given him at his origin for his later evolution. His cosmic childhood would not bear fruit, and would constitute a withering element in him, with the result that he could fall victim to the Luciferic or Ahrimanic hosts and have his independent development taken from him. If the enemies of the human race had brought these efforts to a fully successful conclusion instead of merely to the point of presenting hindrances, the influx of the consciousness soul could have been prevented.

An event in which the inflowing of the spiritual into earthly affairs shows itself particularly clearly is the appearance on the scene and the subsequent destiny of Joan of Arc, the Maid of Orleans (1412-1431). The impulses underlying her actions arise from profoundly unconscious soul depths as far as any awareness on her part is concerned. She follows obscure promptings of the spiritual world. Confusion reigns as a means of keeping the consciousness-soul period from entering. Michael has to prepare his later mission from the realm of the spiritual, and he finds this possible wherever human souls take up his impulses. The Maid's soul is receptive in this sense. Michael works similarly through many other such souls, though in their case that is possible only to a lesser degree, and is historically less conspicuous. He encounters Ahrimanic opposition in just such events as the war between France and England.

In the previous contemplation we discussed the Luciferic opponent whom Michael encounters during this period. But this enemy is further, and most clearly, revealed in the events following upon the appearance of the Maid of Orleans.

It is evident in these events that people did not know what attitude to take with respect to the intervention of the spiritual world in human affairs, an intervention readily grasped by, and absorbed into, the will life of human beings when imaginative understanding was still in existence. To relate to such intervention was no longer possible when the intellectual soul had had its day and no relationship to the consciousness soul had as yet developed. In fact, it has still not been achieved to the present day.

So it came about that the shaping of Europe by the spiritual world at that time came about without human beings having any grasp of what was going on, or being able to exert any influence on the shaping process.

We need only consider what would have happened in the fifteenth century if there had not been a Maid of Orleans to see the significance of this spiritually ordained event. There are those who like to explain such a phenomenon materialistically. It is impossible to reach any understanding with them because they insist on interpreting obviously spiritual matters from a materialistic viewpoint.

Certain of humanity's spiritual strivings also make clearly evident how difficult it had become for men to find their way to the divine-spiritual. Difficulties of this kind simply did not exist during the period when insight could still be attained through imaginations. To form a correct concept of what is meant here, we need only scrutinize those individuals who appeared on the scene as philosophers and thinkers. A philosopher cannot be considered solely on the basis of the influence he exerted on his time, or of the numbers of those who took up his ideas. Rather is he the *expression* of his age, its personified manifestation. The philosopher advances in his ideas what the great majority of mankind harbors unconsciously as an attitude of soul, as unconscious feelings and life impulses. Like a thermometer registering the level of warmth of its surroundings, he indicates the state of soul of the age he lives in. Philosophers are no more the cause of the outlook of their time than thermometers are the cause of the level of warmth in the space around them.

Let us look from this angle at the philosopher René Descartes, who lived from 1596 to 1650 and worked when the age of the consciousness soul was already in progress. His connection with the spiritual world—with actual reality—was based on the slender support provided by the experience, "I think, therefore I am." He looked to the ego, the center of the consciousness of selfhood, for the experiencing of reality, and this only to the extent that the consciousness soul makes possible.

Descartes tries to understand everything with the help of the intellect by examining to what extent the certainty of self-awareness guarantees certainty in other matters also. His question, as he examines every truth handed down by history, is, "Is it as self-evident as 'I think, therefore I am'?" If he can answer, "Yes," then he accepts it.

Does not thinking of this nature shut out the spirit from any and all contemplation of the world content? The manifestation of that spirit has narrowed itself down to the meagerest support in self-awareness; everything else presents itself *immediately* without revealing a trace of spirit. The light of that spirit's revelation, issuing from the intellect in the consciousness soul, can fall only indirectly on everything outside the bounds of self-awareness.

In the period under consideration, man strives with the most intense longing toward the spiritual world, with a consciousness soul still almost devoid of content. A slender thread of light rays out in that direction.

The beings of the spiritual realm immediately bordering on the earthly world and the souls of men living on earth have a difficult time reaching one another. Extraordinary difficulties stand in the way of human participation in Michael's supersensible preparation for his coming mission.

To understand the nature of *the* mood of soul that came to expression in Descartes, let us compare this philosopher with Augustine, who based his view of man's experience of the spiritual world on the same foundation, judged externally, as Descartes. But in Augustine's case, (he lived from 354-430) this was done by resorting to the full imaginative power of the intellectual soul. People rightly see similarity in Augustine's and Descartes' outlook. Augustine's intellect is, however, a remnant of cosmic mind, whereas, in Descartes' case, intellect has already begun to make its way into the individual soul. It is just in the ongoing development of spiritual striving from Augustine to Descartes that we can see how the cosmic character of the thinking powers disappears, to reappear in the individual soul. But we see at the same time how Michael and the human soul find each other in a way that, even though it is attended by difficulties, enables Michael to direct in man what he formerly directed in the cosmos.

The Luciferic and Ahrimanic forces actively oppose this coming together. Lucifer's desire is to allow only those aspects to flourish in man that were his at the time of his cosmic childhood. Ahriman, who both opposes and yet co-operates with the Luciferic forces, would like to permit the evolution of only those powers that were acquired in much more recent times, letting man's cosmic childhood wither.

Under such conditions of aggravated difficulty the souls of men in Europe absorbed the spiritual impulses inherent in ancient world-conceptions brought from the East into the Western world by the Crusades.

Michaelic forces lived most strongly in these ideas. The cosmic intelligence, which Michael had of old been charged with administering, dominated these world conceptions.

How could they be absorbed, considering the abyss separating the forces of the spiritual world from human souls? They entered the consciousness soul when it was only just beginning to develop, encountering, on one hand, the problem of its weak development. Their effect was to drown out its activity, to paralyze it. But, on the other hand, they no longer had to deal with a consciousness based on imaginations. Human souls could not relate to them with full understanding, and they were absorbed either superficially or with a superstitious reaction.

This state of mind must be taken into account if, on the one hand, we want to understand the trends of thought associated with men such as Wycliff and Huss, etc., and the designation 'Rosicrucians,' on the other.

*

GUIDELINES

1. At the beginning of the consciousness-soul age, the intellectual capacities of the human soul had developed to only a slight degree. What the soul longs for in its unconscious depths cannot establish a relationship with what the forces of the region in which Michael dwells could have offered it.

2. This inability to establish a relationship generated enhanced opportunity for the Luciferic powers to keep man from progressing beyond the stage of cosmic childhood and to direct his further development along Luciferic lines, *rather than* to let him proceed on the path ordained by the divine-spiritual forces to which he had been related from the time of his origin.

3. There is further enhanced opportunity for the Ahrimanic powers to cut man off from the forces of his cosmic childhood and to draw him into their own realm for his future evolution.

4. Due to the fact that the Michaelic forces were nevertheless at work, neither of these possibilities was realized.

Mankind's spiritual evolution, however, had to continue under the hindering influences thus created, and *for that reason* took the course it has thus far traveled.

XII

CONTINUATION OF THE SECOND CONTEMPLATION: HELPS AND HINDRANCES TO MICHAEL'S FORCES AT THE TIME OF THE DAWNING OF THE CONSCIOUSNESS SOUL

The embodying of the consciousness soul brought with it a disturbance, felt throughout Europe, of everything that had to do with the religious confessions and matters of ritual. We see this disturbance clearly forecast at the turn of the eleventh century in the advancing of so-called 'proofs of the existence of God,' a movement in which Anselm of Canterbury figured largely. All sorts of intellectual reasons were employed to prove that God exists.

A yearning of this kind could make itself felt only when the earlier way of actually experiencing *God* with one's own soul powers had begun to weaken, for no one feels impelled to produce logical proof of what he thus experiences.

The earlier way was to perceive beings endowed with intelligence—up to God Himself—in one's soul; the new way was the intellectual one of developing thoughts about the 'First Causes' of the universe. The basis for the former was the Michaelic forces, present in the spiritual realm immediately bordering on the earthly world, whereby souls were endowed with capacities beyond those of thoughts directed to sensory experience, capacities that enabled them to attain direct perception of the cosmic beings of intelligence. The second way depended on developing a direct union of the soul with the Michaelic forces.

In matters of worship, broad areas of religious experience, including even so central a sacrament as that of communion, began to be shaken; Wycliff in fifteenth century England and Huss in Bohemia were among those involved in this development. Communion had become a sacrament in which man could connect himself with the spiritual world opened to him by the Christ; for he was able so to unite his being with that of Christ that the fact of physical union was at the same time spiritual fact.

It was possible for the intellectual soul consciousness to picture this union, for the soul still entertained concepts of spirit and matter that saw them so closely related that the one, matter, could be pictured undergoing transition into the other, spirit. Ideas of this sort are, however, not of that intellectual kind that sought proof of God's existence, but rather ideas still possessing some remnant of imagination. They were such that one could perceive in matter the active spirit, and in the spirit sense the striving toward material expression. Ideas of *this* kind have the cosmic Michaelic powers behind them.

Just think how much of what human souls felt to be their holiest, innermost experience grew shaky for them during this period! Personalities—Huss, Wycliff and others among them—in whom the consciousness-soul nature shone out most radiantly, whose state of soul was such as to unite them with the Michaelic forces to a degree attainable for others only centuries later, appeared on the scene. They used the mature powers of the consciousness soul that grew out of hearing the voice of Michael in their hearts to lift themselves to a grasp of the profoundest religious mysteries. They felt that the intellectuality coming in with the consciousness soul must be capable of bringing into their ideas what had been reached in earlier times through imagination.

In contrast to this, the old traditional stance of the human soul had lost all its inner liveliness for the great majority of men. What is called historically, 'the disorders of faith,' which preoccupied the great councils attempting reform in the period when the consciousness soul was beginning to function, is connected with the life of those human beings who did not as yet sense the presence of the consciousness

70

soul within them, but who were also incapable of deriving inner strength and certainty from what remained to them of the intellectual soul.

We can truly say that historic human experiences such as those underlying the councils of Constance and Basel are evidence that the intellectuality seeking its way to man was streaming down from above, from the spiritual world. They also show us an earthly scene in which the intellectual soul was no longer suited to the times. The Michaelic forces hover between the two realms, looking back at their past connection with the divine-spiritual, looking down upon the human kingdom, which also once belonged to the divine world. But mankind now has to enter a sphere, where Michael can offer his help from the spirit, but help with which he must not unite himself. We find in this Michaelic struggle, which is *necessary* in cosmic evolution, but nevertheless means an upsetting of balance in the cosmos, the background of what mankind had to go through at that time with respect to its experience of the holiest truths.

We see deep into the characteristics of that period when we turn our attention to Cardinal Nicholas Cusanus (who is discussed in my book, *Mysticism at the Dawn of the Modern Age*). His personality is like a monument to his time. It was his desire to further general acceptance of an outlook that would not attack wrongs in the physical world in a visionary spirit but rather rely on people's healthy common sense to put back on the right track whatever had gone awry. Anyone who studies the part he played at the Council of Basel and elsewhere in his religious jurisdiction will see how true this is.

If Cusanus here shows himself fully sympathetic to the evolutionary change evidencing itself as the consciousness soul developed, one also finds him manifesting views that give shining witness to the forces of Michael. He brings alive for his time the good ideas of old that had awakened human souls to a feeling for developing capacities whereby the cosmic beings of intelligence could be perceived when Michael was still regent of divine intellectuality. By the 'learned ignorance' of which he speaks is meant insight on a level above the one that perceives the world of the senses, insight that leads thinking beyond intellectuality—ordinary knowing—into a region where the spiritual is grasped—in an 'ignorance' compensated for by actually experienced vision.

Cusanus is thus the personality who, feeling in his own soul life the disturbance of cosmic balance brought about by Michael, tried his intuitive best to turn this disturbance in a direction that would make a contribution to human welfare.

Another element lived, hidden, alongside what was thus spiritually manifest. A few individuals who had a feeling for and grasp of the situation of the Michaelic forces in the cosmos wanted to prepare their soul powers in such a way that they might consciously enter the spiritual realm bordering on the earthly world, where Michael was carrying on his efforts for the human race.

They sought to balance this spiritual undertaking by behaving professionally and in other external respects in such a manner that their way of life appeared no different from that of other people. Due to the fact that they carried out their earthly responsibilities in a perfectly ordinary, loving way, they felt free to devote the inner man to the spiritual task described. Their activities in this direction were the private concern of those thus "secretly" united. What happened on the physical plane seemed to remain untouched by this spiritual striving. But it was all essential to bringing souls into the necessary connection with Michael's world. It was not a question of "secret societies" in the sense of anything undesirable, or that shunned the light of day by remaining hidden. It was rather a coming together of men who became convinced in finding each other that those belonging to their circle had a true awareness of the mission of Michael. Individuals who worked together in this way simply did not talk of their work in the presence of people who might disturb it for lack of understanding. Tasks of this kind were carried out in spiritual movements that ran their course beyond the earthly realm, in the spiritual world bordering it but sending its impulses into life on earth.

Reference is made here to spiritual work that was being done by people living in the physical world but working in unison with beings of the world of spirit who neither enter nor incarnate on the physical plane. We refer to what the world calls—with little justification in fact—the Rosicrucians. True Rosicrucianism was wholly aligned with the activity being carried on by the Michaelic mission; it helped to prepare on earth what Michael was preparing as his spiritual task for a later period.

What this accomplished can be gauged by considering the following.

The characterized difficulties, indeed, the impossibility, of Michael's working directly on human souls were connected with the fact that he wishes to avoid bringing his own being into any contact whatsoever with present-day physical earthly life. He wants to remain in the context of forces that prevail for spiritual beings of his own kind and that prevailed *in the past* for human beings. Any contact with the elements with which man *necessarily* comes in touch in his present-day physical life on earth he *could* only regard as a defiling of his nature.

Now, in man's ordinary life, the soul's spiritual experience, of course, takes effect on physical earthly life, and the latter reacts in turn upon the former. Such reactions express themselves in human moods and in this or that orientation toward the earthly. Interaction of this kind occurs as a rule—though not invariably—in the case of people in public office. The obstacles placed in the way of Michael's work were, therefore, most considerable, indeed, for those intent upon reform.

Difficulties stemming from this quarter were overcome by the Rosicrucians by keeping their external life and its earthly duties quite separate from their work with Michael. When Michael projected his impulse into what a Rosicrucian had prepared his soul to receive from him, he found himself in no danger of becoming involved with earthly matters, for these were excluded from the relationship between Michael and the Rosicrucians by the state of soul cultivated by them.

Genuine Rosicrucian striving thereby provided Michael with the earthly channel for his approaching mission for the earth.

*

GUIDELINES

1. At the start of the consciousness-soul age, man's emancipated intellectuality gravitated toward coming to grips with truth in matters of religious faith and ritual. This could not fail to upset human soul life. People wanted logical proof in questions of essential reality that had previously been directly experienced by the human soul. They sought to apply logical deduction to the content of rituals that could only be imaginatively grasped, and even tried to shape them accordingly.

2. All this is connected with the fact that Michael must avoid any possible contact with the present physical world, on which *man has* to set foot, but that he has nevertheless to continue conveying to human souls the cosmic intellectuality, of which he was the regent in the past. The Michaelic forces thus bring about a disturbance of cosmic balance *essential* to ongoing world evolution.

3. Michael's mission is made easier by the fact that certain individuals, the genuine Rosicrucians, arrange their external life in such a way that it exerts no influence on their inner life of soul. This enables them to develop inner powers whereby they work spiritually with Michael without exposing him to the danger of becoming involved in earthly events, something that would be impossible for him.

XIII

THIRD CONTEMPLATION:
MICHAEL'S SORROW OVER HUMANITY'S EVOLUTION
BEFORE THE START OF HIS EARTHLY ACTIVITY

In the further advance of the consciousness-soul age, the possibility of Michael's relating to mankind in general grows ever more restricted. Intellectuality, now become human capacity, takes over the souls of men, while the imaginative orientation that once enabled them to contemplate the cosmic beings of intelligence disappears. Only in the final third of the nineteenth century does Michael find it possible to begin approaching man. Prior to that time, the path sought by true Rosicrucians provided the only possible approach.

Man now examines nature with his budding intellect. He sees a physical and etheric world that lies outside him. As he acquires a picture of the outside world with the help of the great ideas of Copernicus and Galileo, he loses any concept of himself. He looks at himself, but without any possibility of arriving at a grasp of *what* he is.

An element that is destined to be the bearer of his intelligence now awakens in the depths of his being. His ego joins forces with this element. Now he bears within him a threefold nature. First, there is in his soul-spiritual being—appearing as physical and etheric form—that which, with the Saturn and Sun periods and continuing ever since, has given him his alliance with the divine-spiritual realm. This is where mankind and Michael can unite.

Second, man bears within him his later physical-etheric nature, which he acquired during the Moon and Earth periods. All this is the work and activity of the divine-spiritual, no longer livingly present in it.

It becomes fully livingly present again, however, when the Christ passes through the Mystery of Golgotha. Christ can be found in what is spiritually at work in man's physical and etheric bodies.

Third, man bears within himself that part of his soul and spiritual being that has taken on new aspects during the Moon and Earth periods. Michael has remained active in this part of man's being, whereas he has become increasingly inactive in the part turned toward the Moon and Earth. In that part, it is he who preserved man's divine-human image for him.

He was able to do this until the consciousness-soul age dawned. Then man's entire soul-spiritual entelechy was absorbed into the physical-etheric in order to bring forth the consciousness soul there.

Man's consciousness now began to be lit by what his physical and etheric bodies could tell him about physical and etheric aspects of the natural world around him, while what his ego and astral body could tell him about themselves faded from his ken.

There came a period during which humanity began to feel that its insight no longer sufficed for understanding itself. This gave rise to a search for knowledge about human nature. But the present afforded no possibility of satisfaction. People looked back to earlier periods of history. Humanism appears on the scene as the human mind develops. Humanism was not the product of possessing man, but of having lost him. Had Erasmus of Rotterdam and others like him really possessed man, their activity would have been characterized by a totally different nuance of soul than that given it by humanism.

Still later, Goethe found in Faust a human figure that had entirely lost its humanness.

The 'search for man' grew ever more urgent. The only choice remaining was either to blunt the desire to feel out one's own nature or else to develop the yearning for such insight as an inevitable component of one's soul life.

76

Up to the beginning of the nineteenth century and beyond it, we see the finest minds in all the various areas of European learning and culture developing ideas—historical, scientific, philosophical and mystical—that all represent a striving to discover *man* in a world-outlook grown merely intellectualistic.

The Renaissance, spiritual rebirth, humanism, all hurry—indeed, storm—toward spirituality in a direction in which it *cannot* be found, while impotence, illusion and torpidity obscure the direction in which it must be sought. Meanwhile, the Michaelic forces break through everywhere: in art, in learning, in man himself, but not as yet into the budding powers of the consciousness soul. Spiritual life totters. Michael directs all his forces backward in cosmic evolution in order to gain strength to keep the 'dragon' beneath his feet in balance. The great creations of the Renaissance come into being just in the midst of this mighty exercise of Michaelic power. But they are a refreshening by Michael of the intellectual soul element rather than products of the activity of new soul forces.

Michael can be seen in deep anxiety over whether he can keep up his fight against the 'dragon' when he perceives men trying onesidedly to develop a concept of man from their newly acquired picture of the natural world. He sees them observing nature and attempting to derive a picture of the human being from what they call the laws of nature. He sees them thinking that some animal characteristic becomes more developed, some organ complex functions more smoothly, and that this evolves into man. But to the spiritual gaze of Michael, *man* is not the outcome, for it is a mere 'thought' that thinks out this perfecting and smoother functioning; no one can see it becoming a reality, since it never does.

So people go on living with thoughts about man that are unreal concepts, pure illusion; they pursue a picture of man that they believe they have discovered, but there is actually nothing in their field of observation. "The spiritual sun force shines on their souls; Christ is active. But they cannot as yet give this their attention. Consciousness-soul energy burgeons in their bodies, but doesn't yet want to enter their souls." Such is the nature of the inspiration Michael can be heard expressing in sore anxiety. The question is whether illusion may not so strengthen the 'dragon' that Michael will find it impossible to maintain balance.

Other individuals try with capacities of a more inward and artistic kind to see man and nature as a whole. Goethe uttered tremendous words as he was characterizing Winkelmann's work in a glorious book: "When man's healthy nature works in wholeness, when he senses himself to be in a world that is a single, great, meaningful, precious entity, when a feeling of harmonious well-being affords him an experience of pure, free delight, then the universe, if it were self-aware, would feel that it had arrived at its goal and marvel, rejoicing at this high point of its own nature and becoming." The flaming spirituality that inspired Lessing, the ensouling impulse in Herder's grandiose world view, both echo in these words of Goethe, and all Goethe's own creating is a many-faceted revelation of the same spirit. Schiller, in his *Letters on Aesthetics*, gives a description of ideal man, who embraces the universe within himself as Goethe said, and builds reality of it in concert with his fellowmen.

But where does *this* picture of the human being shining like the morning sun over a springtime earth come from?

It is something that made its way into human feeling as a result of studying Grecian man. People cherished it with a strong Michaelic impulse, but could nurture this impulse only by turning their attention back to antiquity. When Goethe tried to express what man was, he felt himself in starkest conflict with the consciousness soul. He sought it in Spinoza's philosophy. He thought for the first time that he had glimpsed man truly while he was on his journey to Italy and was concerning himself with Grecian culture. In the last analysis, he takes flight from the consciousness soul emerging in Spinoza and returns to the fading intellectual soul. All he can do is to bring an unlimited infusion of this into the consciousness soul in his all-embracing view of nature.

Michael looks gravely upon this search for the human being also. An element that he can feel for enters here into humanity's spiritual evolution; it is *the same* human being who once perceived the essence of intelligent being when Michael was its cosmic regent. But this same human element would be lost to Michael's sphere of action and fall under Lucifer's rule were it not taken hold of by the spiritualized energy of the consciousness soul. The other great concern in Michael's life is that Lucifer might gain the upper hand in the disturbed cosmic spiritual balance.

Michael's preparation for his mission at the end of the nineteenth century goes forward in a mood of cosmic tragedy. On the earth beneath, deepest satisfaction is often felt over the outcome of man's conceiving of nature, but in Michael's realm there is a tragic sense of the obstacles hindering the growth of a true picture of the human being.

In earlier periods, Michael's lofty, spiritualized love lived in the raying out of sunlight, in the gleam of the morning skies and in the stars' sparkling. Now this love had taken on as its dominant trait a sorrowing gaze bent upon the human race.

Michael's cosmic situation became one of tragic difficulty but also one demanding solution, just at the period immediately preceding his mission on the earth. Human beings could maintain intellectuality only in the bodily realm, and there, only in the senses. On the one hand, they therefore excluded from any attempt at understanding everything that did not derive from sensory experience; nature became for them a realm restricted to what the senses could reveal of it, and these revelations were wholly materially conceived. Nature's creations were no longer looked upon as the work of the divine-spiritual, but rather as something simply in existence, lacking spirit, yet of which it was asserted that it had brought forth the spiritual element in which man lives. On the other hand, people wanted to accept only such aspects of the spiritual world as had become matters of historical record. Spiritual scrutinizing of the past, as well as of the present, was vigorously repudiated.

All that still lived in the human soul was drawn from current realms of experience that Michael did not enter. People were delighted to feel 'firm' ground underfoot. They thought they had achieved this because they did not seek in nature concepts perhaps tinged by the subjective fantasy they so feared. But Michael was not happy; he had to carry on the battle against Lucifer and Ahriman in his own world, remote from humanity. This resulted in his great and tragic difficulty, for Lucifer's approach to man is made the easier the more Michael, who is also a preserver of the past, is forced to keep at a distance from humanity. So Michael, for the sake of mankind, waged a fierce battle with Ahriman and Lucifer in the spiritual world immediately bordering on the earth, while men on earth occupied their souls in ways that ran counter to their own wholesome evolution.

All the above applies, of course, only to the spiritual life of Europe and America. It would be necessary to speak quite differently about Asia.

*

GUIDELINES

1. In the earliest period of the consciousness soul's development, man had the feeling that the imaginatively conveyed picture he had had of the human race and of his own nature had been lost to him. Since he was as yet powerless to find it in the consciousness soul, he tried to discover it by natural scientific or historical means. He longed to have restored to him his earlier image of what a human being is.

80

2. This led, not to a true being filled with humanness, but only to illusions. This fact went unnoticed, however, and people felt themselves to be on solid ground.

3. Michael was therefore forced to look with sorrow and concern upon mankind's development during the period preceding his assumption of his earthly task. For men turned their backs on any contemplation of things spiritual, thereby cutting themselves off from everything that might have joined them to Michael.

XIV

CHRISTMAS CONTEMPLATION:
THE LOGOS MYSTERY

The Mystery of Golgotha lent its illuminating rays to our study of the Michael Mystery. That was conditioned by the fact that Michael is that beneficent power whereby man is guided to the Christ.

But the mission of Michael is such that it takes place repeatedly, in rhythmical succession, in the course of humanity's cosmic development. Its beneficent influence on earthly man was experienced again and again prior to the Mystery of Golgotha. It was connected with everything that the still extra-earthly Christ power was actively engaged in bringing about on earth for the sake of mankind's evolution. After the Mystery of Golgotha it began serving Christ in what He intends to accomplish for earthly humanity. It reoccurs in ever-changing and evolving form, but nevertheless as repetition.

In contrast to this, the Mystery of Golgotha is a cosmic event of superlative importance that occurs only *once* in the entire course of man's cosmic evolution.

The ever-threatening danger of man's separation from divine-spiritual being, to which he was predestined from the beginning, first became fully actual at the time when humanity was coming into its intellectual soul development.

What we nowadays call 'nature' emerged round about man in proportion to the degree to which his soul lost the ability to participate in the experience of divine-spiritual beings.

Man no longer perceived his own humanity in the divine-spiritual universe; instead, he looked upon the earthly works of the divine-spiritual. But he did not as yet see these in the abstract form to which we are presently accustomed; that is, as physical creatures and occurrences linked by those abstract conceptual contents known as "natural laws." He saw them as a divine-spiritual element, an element in rhythmical movement, of which he became aware in the flourishing and decline of animal life, in the sprouting and growth of vegetation, in the flowing of springs and rivers, in winds and cloud formation. All these living creatures and processes round about him were for his feeling deeds and gestures, the speech of the divine being that underlies the world of *nature*.

Just as there was once a time when man looked upon the positions and movements of the stars as the deeds and gestures of cosmic divinities and read their messages therein, so, now, the "facts of nature" came to be seen as expressions of the earth goddess—for the divinity acting in natural events was conceived of as feminine.

Remnants of this picturing of things were an imaginative content that saturated the intellectual soul and lived on within the souls of men well into the Middle Ages.

Knowledgeable people spoke of the deeds of the 'goddess' when they explained "natural happenings." This living, inwardly ensouled way of viewing nature became incomprehensible to humanity with the gradual strengthening of the consciousness soul.

This way of looking at things in the intellectual soul era calls to mind the myth of Persephone and the mystery reflected in it.

Persephone, the daughter of Demeter, is forced by the god of the underworld to return with him to his kingdom. It is ultimately agreed that she must spend only half of every year there, the other half in the upper world.

This myth still gives powerful, grandiose expression to the way men of the ancient past understood, in dream-like clairvoyance, the earth's whole process of becoming.

In the beginning, all cosmic activity proceeded from the earth's surroundings. The earth itself was only just coming into being. It built up its being in the cosmic evolutionary process from the forces active in its environment. The divine-spiritual beings of the cosmos were the creative powers at work in its development.—When it had advanced to the point of becoming an independent cosmic body, a divine-spiritual element made its way down to it from out of the cosmos and became an earthly divinity. The dream-like clairvoyance of early man brought him knowledge of this cosmic fact; the Persephone myth was a relict of it. Another such relict was the way men sought, right down into the Middle Ages, to acquire an understanding of 'nature.' What men sought after was not yet what the senses conveyed, that is, the surface appearances of earthly things, but rather the forces working toward the surface from earth's depths. These 'forces of the depths,' these 'underworld' forces, were perceived in their interaction with the workings of the stars and of the elements environing the earth.

A great variety of plant growth confronts us, revealed in a brilliant show of color. Forces of sun, moon and stars all work together here with forces from terrestrial depths. These forces derive from minerals, whose presence must be attributed to the fact that cosmic beings have given themselves to the earth. That stone juts forth from the 'underworld' is because heavenly powers have become earthly. Animals, however, have not taken on the forces of earth's depths. They originate wholly from the cosmic forces acting from earth's environment; they owe their growth and development, their ability to absorb nutrients, their mobility, to the sun forces streaming into earth. They possess the faculty to reproduce their kind as a result of the in-streaming forces of the moon. The multiplicity of animal forms and species comes from the manifold way in which the positions of the stars work from the world-all upon animal life and shape it. But the animals have merely been deposited on the earth by the cosmos. The only way they participate in the earth is through their dim life of consciousness. They are not creatures of the earth in origin, growth, or in any of the equipment whereby they are able to perceive and move about.

This grandiose idea of the earth's becoming lived at one time in the awareness of the human race. The remnant of it still in existence in the Middle Ages wears scarcely a trace of its erstwhile grandeur. To achieve any knowledge of it requires going back with clairvoyant vision into most ancient times; even such physical documents as are presently available allow only those possessed of spiritual insight to perceive the soul content of that period.

Now, man is not in a position to keep as aloof from the earth as does the animal. To say this is to touch on the mysteries of both man and animal, mysteries reflected in the animal worship of the ancients, and of the Egyptians in particular. Animals were looked upon as guests of the earth, as creatures in whose nature the beings and activity of the spiritual world bordering on the physical could be perceived. In mingling animal and human forms and making images of them, people brought to light the shapes of those in-between elemental beings who, in the course of world evolution, are on the way to becoming human beings, but who keep from becoming men by not entering the earthly realm. Such beings exist, and the Egyptians who made images of them were merely reproducing what they had clairvoyantly beheld. But beings of this kind do not possess man's full self-awareness. To attain that, man had to enter the earthly sphere so completely that he absorbed some of its nature into his own.

He had to be exposed to the fact that what he perceives in this earthly world, though it is the product of divine-spiritual beings with whom he is linked, is nothing more than their wrought work. Since what he confronts is only their wrought work, their product, detached from its source, Luciferic and Ahrimanic beings have access to it. This imposes upon man the necessity of making this product, pervaded by Lucifer and Ahriman, the scene of the earthly portion of his life's shaping.

This was possible without a permanent detaching of the human element from its divine-spiritual origin so long as man had not yet progressed to the intellectual-soul stage of his development. At that point, a corruption of his physical, etheric and astral being occurred. The science of an earlier time recognized this corruption as something living in man's nature that was essential to an advance of his consciousness to the stage of self-awareness. In the knowledge cultivated in the places dedicated to learning by Alexander the Great there lived an Aristotelianism that, properly understood, sets forth this corruption as a decisive feature of its psychological teaching. Later on, ideas of this kind were no longer grasped in their inner aspect.

In the times prior to the development of the intellectual soul, man was still so interwoven with the forces of his divine-spiritual origin that they could act from their cosmic sphere to keep in balance the Luciferic and Ahrimanic powers that were besetting man on earth. Man did his part in maintaining this balance when the *image* of the divine-spiritual being was presented, during mystery ceremonials and other rituals, descending into and then triumphantly rising from the realms of Lucifer and Ahriman. So we see in the pre-Mystery of Golgotha era, popular cultic representations in pictorial form of what actually became reality in the Mystery of Golgotha.

When the intellectual soul was undergoing development, human beings could only be protected by reality against detachment from the divine-spiritual beings to whom man belonged. The divine, in the form of an individual entity, had to enter inwardly on the earthly plane into the organization of the intellectual soul, which, while on earth, derived its life from earthly sources. This was achieved by Christ, the divine-spiritual Logos, joining His cosmic destiny, for humanity's sake, to that of earth.

Persephone descended to the earthly realm to save the plant world from having to form itself from earthly elements alone. Hers was the descent of a divine-spiritual being into terrestrial nature. Persephone, too, experiences resurrection of a kind, but in a rhythmical succession, year by year.

This event, a cosmic one that takes place on earth, stands in contrast to the descent of the Logos for mankind's redemption. Persephone descends to restore nature to its original orientation. This has to be based on rhythm since natural processes undergo rhythmical recurrence. The Logos makes its descent into humanity as a one-time happening in mankind's evolution. *This* evolution is only one step in a gigantic cosmic rhythm which,in mankind was something entirely different prior to reaching the human level, and will again, later on, become something entirely different. Plant life, however, repeats itself as such in quite brief rhythms.

To see the Mystery of Golgotha in this light became necessary for humanity at the consciousness-soul stage and, from that point onward, because the detaching of man in the period of his intellectual soul development would already have posed a danger if the Mystery of Golgotha had not occurred. A total darkening of the spiritual world for human consciousness would have had to take place in the consciousness-soul age if that soul were unable to gather strength enough to look back with insight to its divine-spiritual origin. If it can do so, it discovers the cosmic Logos to be that being who can serve as its guide in that rediscovery. It permeates itself with the tremendous picture that reveals what took place on Golgotha.

A loving grasp of the cosmic Christmas celebrated in an annually repeated festival of remembrance forms the beginning of this insight. The consciousness soul, which has gathered to itself the coldest soul element, intellectuality, is strengthened when genuine love is allowed to flow into it. This is that warmth of love that pours out in its loftiest form when directed toward the child Jesus as he appears on earth in the holy night of the cosmic Christmas. It enables man to let earth's greatest spiritual event, which was a physical event as well, work upon his soul; he has begun to absorb the Christ into his being.

Nature must come to be known in a way that allows us to see Persephone, or the being called Nature that was still perceived in the early part of the Middle Ages—as the eternal, divine-spiritual power of nature's origin, out of which the natural basis of man's earthly existence arose and constantly receives renewal.

Man's world must be grasped as revealing in Christ the primal, eternal Logos, who works in the realm of the divine-spiritual being linked with man from the beginning toward the development of man's spiritual human nature.

To turn human hearts in love toward these great cosmic connections is the proper goal of that festival of remembrance annually engaged in by man as he contemplates the cosmic Christmas. If love of this kind lives in human hearts, it pours its fire through the frigid light element of the consciousness soul. If the consciousness soul had to do without this fire, man would never achieve its spiritualizing. He would either die of the chill of the intellectual soul or remain standing in a life of the spirit that would fail to advance to the consciousness soul level. That would mean coming to a halt at the stage of intellectual soul development.

But coldness is not the real nature of the consciousness soul; it only seems so *at the start* of its unfolding; at that point it can reveal its content of light, but cannot yet manifest the cosmic warmth from which it issues.

To feel and experience Christmas in this way *can make the soul aware of how the glory of the divine-spiritual beings revealed by their images in the wide starry world is proclaimed to man, and how he is delivered in his life on earth from those beings who desire to estrange him from his origin.*

*

GUIDELINES

1. The activity on behalf of cosmic and human evolution engaged in by Michael and his hosts is *rhythmically repeated*, though in ever-changing and progressive form, before and after the Mystery of Golgotha.

89

2. The Mystery of Golgotha is a one-time event, as well as the greatest event in the evolution of the human race. We cannot speak in this instance of a rhythmical repetition. Even though this evolution of the human race is part of a mighty cosmic rhythm, it is nevertheless the one overarching *single* element within that rhythm. Before it became this single element, the human race was something basically different from a human race and will later undergo a change into something else again. We may say that many Michaelic events take place in the evolution of humanity, but only one Event of Golgotha.

3. The divine-spiritual being that descends into earthly depths in order to spiritualize the processes in nature accomplishes this in the rapid rhythmical repetition of the yearly cycle. It brings about the ensouling of nature with primal, eternal forces, just as the Christ Who came down to earth brings about the ensouling of humanity with the primal, eternal Logos, destined to work unceasingly for the salvation of mankind.

XV

HEAVENLY HISTORY. MYTHOLOGICAL HISTORY. EARTHLY HISTORY. THE MYSTERY OF GOLGOTHA.

The cosmic expanses and the earth's center confront one another in the spatial universe. The stars are, as we say, "scattered" in cosmic space, while, from the earth's center, forces ray out in every direction into that space.

According to the way man looks at the universe in the present cosmic era, the stars' shining and the action of earth's forces can only appear to be the collective work of those divine-spiritual beings with whom he is inwardly connected.

But there was once a cosmic era in which that shining and those earthly forces were still the immediate revelation of divine-spiritual beings, and in his dim consciousness man felt them active within *his* being.

Then came another age. The starry heavens as corporeal being fell away from the influence of the divine-spiritual. What one might call a world spirit and a world body came into existence. The world spirit was a multiplicity of divine-spiritual beings. In the past era they directed their activity onto the earth from their stations in the stars. What shone from the great expanses of the universe and the forces radiating from earth's center were in reality the intelligence and the will of divine-spiritual beings at work in the creating of the earth and its human populations.

In the cosmic epoch that followed upon the Saturn and Sun development, the activity of intelligence and will of these divine-spiritual beings grew ever more spiritually inward. The 'world body,' the harmonious ordering of the stars in universal space, was structured by their original active presence. Looking back at all this with spiritual vision, we can say that the world spirit and the world body came into

91

being out of the primal spirit body of these world creating beings. The corporeal universe bears witness, in the arrangement of the stars and in their movement, to the intelligence and will-inspired working of the gods in that past age. But what was once freely creative, mobile divine will and intelligence in the stars' movement has become subject, in the cosmic present, to fixed natural law.

So we may say that what we see presently shining down upon us here on earth from the starry worlds is no longer the immediate expression of the gods' will and intelligence, but instead a fixed record of their former activity in the stars. We therefore see in the star patterns of the heavens that evoke such marvelling in the human soul a past rather than a present revelation of the gods.

But what is of the past in starlight is of the present in the spiritual world; man lives with his being in this present world spirit.

In the matter of the world's shaping, we have to look back to an ancient cosmic epoch in which the world spirit and the world body worked as one. Then we have an intermediate epoch, a period in which the two worked as a duo. For the future, we have to conceive a third epoch in which the world spirit will again include the world body in its functioning.

It would not have been possible to make any calculations relative to the constellations and star orbits in the ancient epoch; they were then an expression of the free intelligence and free will activity of divine-spiritual beings. In the future, they will again become incalculable.

'Calculations' are significant for the intermediate period only.

What is true of the constellations and star orbits applies also to the functioning of the forces that radiate from the earth's center into cosmic space. This working 'out-of-the-depths' also goes through a calculable phase.

But everything moves from that ancient cosmic epoch

toward the intermediate one, in which space and time became calculable and the divine-spiritual as the revelation of intelligence and will has to be sought beyond the domain of the 'calculable.'

Only in this intermediate epoch do conditions exist that enable man to progress from a dim state of consciousness to clear, free self-awareness and the use of his own free intelligence, his own free will.

The time had to come when Copernicus and Kepler 'calculated' the physical universe. Man's self-awareness had first to be developed by the cosmic forces responsible for the shaping of this epoch. The groundwork for this self-awareness was laid in an earlier period. Then the moment came when that consciousness was sufficiently developed to undertake calculations of universal space.

Earthly 'history' now begins. This could not have happened had cosmic space not become fixed in the patterns and orbits of the stars. The 'course of earthly history' is a reflection—albeit a metamorphosed one—of what was once upon a time 'cosmic history.'

Older peoples still retained awareness of this 'cosmic history.' They paid more attention to it than they did to earthly history.

'Earthly history' reflected the exercise of man's intelligence, first, in conjunction with the cosmic will and intelligence of the gods, then later independently of them.

'Heavenly history' reflected the life of will and intelligence of the divine-spiritual beings with whom man is connected.

Looking back at the spiritual life of the various peoples, we come to a remote past in which men were so aware of having a common existence and common will with the divine-spiritual beings that their own history is, at the same time, cosmic history. When a person spoke of his own 'origin,' he was recounting cosmic rather than earthly events. Even in the case of his own momentary life, what went on in his earthly environment appeared so insignificant compared to cosmic happenings that his attention was given to them rather than to the earthly.

There was a time when humanity consciously beheld heavenly history in mighty visions, wherein the divine-spiritual beings appeared before men's souls. They spoke, and men heard in inspired dreaming what they said. They revealed their forms, and men beheld them in dream-like imaginations.

This heavenly history, which filled men's souls for a long time, was followed by the mythical history that is presently considered by so many people to be merely ancient poetry. This history linked cosmic happenings with earthly events. It speaks, for example, of 'heroes,' who are supersensible beings of a higher development than that of man. During a certain evolutionary period, for example, man had as yet developed only as far as the sentient soul, whereas the 'hero' had already advanced to the point of possessing a spirit self. A 'hero' cannot incarnate directly in earthly circumstances, but only indirectly, by descending into the body of a human being and thus becoming able to take part in life as a man among men. The "initiates" of an earlier time were beings of this kind.

In the case of all these events that took place in the world's development, it was not a question of how humanity 'conceived' what happened in successive epochs; the fact was, rather, that changes came about in the relationship between the more spiritual 'incalculable' and the corporeal 'calculable' spheres. But it is true that long after circumstances changed, various peoples clung in their minds to a world outlook corresponding to much earlier phases of reality. The situation was first such that their consciousness failed to keep pace with cosmic events and therefore still actually beheld things at an earlier stage. Then came a time when the power of vision faded and what had gone before was retained only as tradition. Thus, for example, people of the Middle Ages traditionally pictured an interchange between the heavenly world and the earthly world that they no longer witnessed, since imaginative vision was no more.

Then, too, the earth's various populations developed unevenly, some clinging longer, some more briefly to this or that particular view of things, so that world views belonging essentially to consecutive evolutionary phases exist side by side.

But the various ways of looking at things do not stem from this fact alone. They may also be ascribed to the different ways in which different peoples were disposed to view things. Thus, for example, the Egyptians beheld the world of beings whose development to the stage of humanness had been prematurely arrested, so that they did not become human beings, and they made it their concern to follow what a person did in company with these beings in his life after death. The Chaldeans tended rather to perceive how good or evil extraterrestrial beings entered into the life of earth and participated in it.

The first, exceedingly long-lasting epoch of 'heavenly history' was followed by the epoch of 'mythological history,' which, in turn, was shorter, but still long in comparison with the later period of earthly history.

People found it difficult, as I have shown, to give up that early view of things in which gods and men were regarded as working in close communion. So 'true earthly history' made its appearance long ago, with the development of the intellectual soul, but people still went on 'thinking' along past lines. Only with the first budding of the consciousness soul did they begin to turn their attention to 'real' history. People started to experience independent intelligence and free will in the 'history' that proceeded from human spirits detached from the divine-spiritual.

The world events with which man is interwoven thus ran their course between the fully calculable and the working of independent intelligence and free will. They are seen in all possible intermediate stages between the two extremes.

Man lives his life between birth and death with the calculable providing the physical basis for the development of the incalculable in his free, inner soul-spiritual life. He lives his life between death and rebirth in the incalculable, but in such a manner that the calculable develops in thought form in the inwardness of his soul-spiritual existence. He thus builds his coming earthly life out of the calculable element.

The incalculable lives itself out on earth in 'history,' though it has a weak admixture of the calculable in it.

The Luciferic and Ahrimanic beings actively oppose themselves to the order established through the interworking of the calculable and the incalculable by the divine-spiritual beings with whom man has been linked from the beginning; they are against the harmonizing of the cosmos by 'measure, weight and number.' Lucifer is unable to unite the calculable with the nature he has assumed. His ideal is cosmic unconditioned intelligence and will activity.

This Luciferic tendency is properly operative in those aspects of the world order in which freedom is intended to hold sway. Here, Lucifer fills the proper role of spiritual helper in humanity's evolution. It would not be possible, without his help, for freedom to be introduced into man's soul-spiritual being, based as it is on a calculable bodily foundation. But Lucifer is desirous of extending his tendency over the entire cosmos. So his activity is one of battling against the divine-spiritual order to which man of old belonged.

At this point, Michael intervened. He belongs with his own being to the incalculable element, but he brings about the balance between the incalculable and the calculable, which he bears within him as a cosmic thought received from his gods.

The Ahrimanic powers assume a different stance in the universe. They are the complete opposite of the divine-spiritual beings with whom man was originally connected. At present, these beings are purely spiritual powers, the bearers of perfect, free intelligence and perfectly free will.

But in this intelligence and this free will they develop insight into the necessity of the calculable and the unfree in the form of a world thought, out of which man will emerge to develop into a free being. From their place in the cosmos they are bound in love with the calculable and with that world-thought. This love streams out from them throughout the universe.

Cold hatred for everything developing in freedom lives, in greatest contrast, in the greedy desiring of the Ahrimanic powers. Ahriman's striving tends in the direction of making a cosmic machine out of what he streams outward into universal space from the earth. His sole ideal is 'measure, weight and number.' He was summoned into the cosmos that serves human evolution because it was essential to develop this 'mass, weight and number' realm of his.

Only those who grasp the universe in all its spiritual-corporeal aspects truly comprehend it. This must be taken into account right down into nature itself in considering such forces as those of divine-spiritual beings working out of love and those of Ahriman working out of hatred. We must see in the cosmic warmth of nature that sets in in springtime and continues on into summer the natural love of divine-spiritual beings. In the searing cold of winter, we must become aware of Ahrimanic activity.

At midsummer, Lucifer weaves his power into the natural love, the warmth. At Christmastide, the divine-spiritual beings with whom man was originally connected oppose their strength to Ahriman's frosty hate. Then, as spring approaches, this divine love in nature constantly tempers natural Ahrimanic hatred.

The appearance of this annually recurring divine love is the time of remembrance when the free divine element entered with the Christ into the earthly calculable. Christ works in total freedom in the calculable, thus rendering harmless the Ahrimanic element that craves the calculable alone.

The Event of Golgotha is the free cosmic deed of love in

earth's history. It can only be grasped by the love that man brings to its understanding.

*

GUIDELINES

1. The cosmic process with which man's evolution is bound up and which is reflected in his awareness as 'history' in the most comprehensive sense falls into three sections: The long drawn out period of heavenly history; the less extended period of mythological history; the relatively brief period of earthly history.

2. This cosmic process falls presently into the incalculable working of divine-spiritual beings who create in free intelligence and free will, and into the calculable processes of the world body.

3. The Luciferic powers oppose themselves to the world body's calculable processes, while the Ahrimanic powers work against creativity based on free intelligence and free will.

4. The Event of Golgotha is a free cosmic deed originating in world love and only to be understood by human love.

XVI

WHAT IS REVEALED WHEN WE LOOK BACK
INTO REPEATED EARTHLY LIVES

When we look back with spiritual sight into a person's past earthly lives, we come upon a number of such lives in which the human being involved was already an individual. His external appearance was similar to that of the present, and his inner life had individual character. Some of these lives evidence possession of the intellectual soul, but not as yet of the consciousness soul, and there are other lives in which only the sentient soul was as yet developed.

The above applies to the various epochs of earthly history, and it holds true of even earlier periods as well.

But spiritual perception takes one back to eras in which this was not as yet the case. Men of those eras are discovered to be still closely interwoven with the world of divine-spiritual beings, both as to their inner life and outer conditions. Here, human beings are present as earthly men, but they are not yet detached from divine-spiritual being, thought and will.

In still earlier times, detached humanity is lost sight of entirely, and all that can be seen are divine-spiritual beings within whom human beings live like babes in a womb.

Mankind has passed through these three stages of its evolution during the epochs of its earthly sojourn. The transition from the first into the second took place in the final phase of Lemuria, the transition of the second into the third, in Atlantean times.

Just as contemporary man carries within him memories of his experiences, so is he the bearer of a cosmic memory of everything he has undergone in the ways described. What, actually, is our earthly soul life but a world of memories, ready at all times to add new perceptions? Man lives his inner earthly existence in this interplay of memory and new experience.

But this inner earthly existence could not come into being and develop if there were not still present in man, in the form of cosmic memory, what is perceived on looking back with spiritual vision into the first stage of his earthly human development, when he had not yet been detached from divine-spiritual being.

The only living remnant of what took place in the world during that period is to be found in what develops within man's nerve-sense organism. All the forces operative in external nature at that time have died out since then and are to be observed only in a lifeless form.

Thus there lives in the human thought world as present revelation something which, to exist on earth, has to have as its basis what had already developed in man before he attained individual earthly being.

In his life between death and rebirth, man constantly experiences this stage anew. But he carries into the world of divine-spiritual beings, which again receives him into the same inclusion in which it once contained him, the full measure of that individual existence resulting from his incarnations on the earth. In the period between death and rebirth he is simultaneously both in the present and in all the time he had lived through in the course of his repeated earthly lives, as well as during the repeated periods between death and rebirth.

In regard to man's life of feeling, the case is different. The feeling world relates to experiences immediately following upon those wherein man is not yet individually evident, namely, those experiences undergone by man when, although he had reached the human stage, he was not yet detached from divine-spiritual being, thought and will. Human beings would not be presently able to develop the feeling sphere if it were not for the rhythmical organism on which it is based. Cosmic memory of the second stage of human evolution lives in this organism.

Man's present-day soul life, and an element stemming from a much earlier era that goes on working in him, thus engage in joint activity in his world of feeling.

In the life between death and rebirth, man experiences the content of the time described above as the boundary of his cosmos. The life between death and a new birth is to him spiritually in his existence in the period between his full connection with the divine-spiritual world and his detachment from it, what the starry worlds are to him in his physical earthly life. There, it is not the physical heavenly bodies that appear to him at the world's border but, at every star location, a group of divine-spiritual beings who are that star's reality.

Will alone, rather than thought or feeling, characterizes earth-lives, which observation shows have attained the level of personal individuality. The cosmic element that gives man his external form is preserved therein as cosmic memory, living in the form of forces in man's human shape. These forces are not the forces of the will itself, but of what gives the will forces their foundation in the human organism.

In the life between death and rebirth, this region of man's being is located beyond "the world's border." Man conceives it there as something that will be his own possession again in his next earthly life.

In his nerve-sense system, man is still as connected with the cosmos as he was while still contained in a merely germinal stage within divine-spiritual being.

In his rhythmic system, man still lives today in the same relationship to the cosmos that obtained at the time when he was already on the scene as man, but not as yet detached from the divine-spiritual.

Man lives in the metabolic-limb system, which is the basis of his will activity, with everything working on in it that he has undergone, both in his earthly lives and in his lives between death and rebirth, since the time when he began having personal, individual incarnations.

Man receives from among the forces of the earth only what forms the foundation of his self-awareness. The physical bodily basis of this self-awareness also stems from what the earth has to give; everything else a human being has comes from extraterrestrial, cosmic sources. The feeling and thought supporting astral body, and its etheric basis, all the liveliness of life in the etheric body, indeed, even the physico-chemical action going on in the physical body, are of cosmic origin. Strange as it may seem, the physico-chemical action inside a human being is not of the earth.

That man develops this non-terrestrial, cosmic element in himself is due to the action of the *planets* and of other *stars*. The sun's forces bring to the earth what he thus develops. The human cosmic element is transposed into the earthly realm by the sun's action. Through this, man lives on earth as a heavenly being. The capacity to reproduce his kind, in which he goes beyond the limits of his human shaping, is, however, a gift of the moon.

These are, of course, not the only activities of the sun and moon, which are also responsible for other, profoundly spiritual effects.

When, at Christmastide, the sun takes on ever stronger forces destined for the earth, this is its *rhythmically* repeated yearly activity in the earthly physical and an expression of the spiritual in nature. The evolution of mankind is a single episode in an immense cosmic year. This is evident from the above. Christmas in this cosmic year is that moment when the sun does not merely act upon the earth out of the spirit of nature, but when the soul of the sun, the Christ Spirit, descends to the earth.

Just as every single human being's individual experiences are related to cosmic memory, so do human souls develop the right feeling toward the annually repeated Christmases when they think of the heavenly, cosmic Christ Event as working on, not as a merely human, but as a cosmic memory. It is not only man who thinks festively of Christ's descent at Christmas, but the cosmos participates therein as well.

*

GUIDELINES

1. When we look back into an individual's repeated earthly lives, we find them grouped in three different phases: an earliest phase, wherein man existed in germinal form within the being of the divine-spiritual rather than as an individual. In this viewing of the past one comes upon divine-spiritual beings (the Archai), but not as yet upon human beings.

2. There then follows an intermediate stage, in which man is indeed present as an individual being but is not as yet detached from the thinking and will and life of the divine-spiritual. He still does not possess his present-day personality, which is the product of his having achieved fully independent being in his earthly life, detached from the divine-spiritual world.

3. The third stage is the present one. Man experiences himself in his human shape, detached from the divine-spiritual world, and he feels the world to be an environment that he encounters as an individual, personal entity. This stage begins in Atlantean times.

XVII

FIRST PART OF THE CONTEMPLATION:
WHAT IS REVEALED WHEN WE LOOK BACK
INTO PAST LIVES BETWEEN DEATH AND REBIRTH?

In the previous contemplation we explored the totality of human life in a way that focused our attention on repeated earthly lives. This complementary study which throws still brighter illumination on what the first one revealed, examines the successive lives lived between dying and being born again.

Here, too, we find that the content of these lives in its present-day aspect can be followed back into the past only up to a certain point in the earth's evolution. This content is characterized by the fact of man's carrying through the gates of death the inner strength of a self-awareness garnered from living on the earth. This enables him to relate as an individual to the divine-spiritual beings in whose midst he lives.

This was not the case in the preceding period, when man had not progressed to the necessary point in the development of his self-consciousness. The strength he gained from his life on earth did not suffice to bring about his separation from the divine-spiritual world to a degree that enabled him to live an individual existence between death and rebirth. Though he did not live enclosed within divine-spiritual beings, he was, nevertheless, part of their sphere of action to the extent that his will was essentially their will rather than his own.

This period was preceded by a still earlier one wherein it is not possible to discover any trace of man in his present soul-spiritual state. Looking back, one comes instead upon the world of divine-spiritual beings, the Archai, within whom man is to be found only in a germinal condition.

The fact is that when we look back into a single individual's lives we come, not upon just a single divine-spiritual being, but upon all the beings who comprise that hierarchy.

There lived in these divine-spiritual beings the will that man should come into existence. The will of all was involved in the evolution of every single individual. During that evolutionary period man still lived unformed in the divine-spiritual world, and the cosmic aim of their choral activity was the development of the human form.

It may seem strange that the whole choir of divine-spiritual beings was active on behalf of the single individual. But, even before this period, the hierarchies of the Exusiai, Dynameis, Kyriotetes, Thrones, Cherubim and Seraphim worked in the same way throughout the Moon, Sun and Saturn evolutions to bring forth and develop man.

What evolved on Saturn, Sun and Moon as pre-human beings had dissimilar forms. Some of them were predominantly limb system organisms, others more trunk systems, still others more head systems. Yet, they were all still truly human. They are called pre-human here simply to distinguish them from the man of a later stage in whom all three systems merged in the one human form. A further differentiation, however, can be made in the case of these pre-human beings: we can speak of heart men, lung men, and so on.

The Archai regarded it as their task to merge all these forms of early man—forms whose soul lives corresponded to their one-sidedness—into one common shape.

They took man over from the hands of the Exusiai, who had *in thought* already created a oneness out of the multiplicity of human forms. But this oneness lived in the thought of the Exusiai as an ideal form, as a universal thought. The Archai built this thought into an etheric pattern, but in such a way that it had the generative power to bring forth the physical form.

106

An awesome perspective opens out before the viewer of these facts: The perspective of man as the goal and ideal of the gods. But to become aware of this cannot induce human arrogance and conceit, for *man* can call his own only what he has made of himself, with self-awareness, during his earthly lives. Cosmically considered, this is not a great deal if one compares it with what the gods have created out of the macrocosm—which they themselves are—when they laid the foundation of man's individual being so that he might become the microcosm that he is. The divine-spiritual beings confront one another in the cosmos. The visible expression of this confrontation is the configuration of the starry heavens. It was their will to create a unity of what they are together.

To understand rightly what the hierarchy of the Archai accomplished in their choral creating of the human form, we have to take into account the fact that there is a huge difference between that form and man's physical body. The physical body is that in him that is subject to physico-chemical processes. These run their course inside the human form of present-day man. But that form itself is something profoundly spiritual. It should generate a solemn mood in us to realize that, with physical senses, we perceive in a human form a spiritual reality in the physical world. A person who has developed spiritual vision beholds a real imagination in the human form, an imagination that has descended into the physical world. If one wants to behold imaginations, one has to cross the threshold between the physical world and the neighboring spiritual realm. But in doing so one becomes aware that the human form is related to these imaginations.

As one looks back in soul, observing the lives between death and rebirth, one sees this coming into being of the human form as the first period. It also becomes apparent how deep a relationship exists between man and the hierarchy of the Archai.

We can already speak of a first intimation, in this period, of the distinction between lives lived on earth and those lived between death and rebirth. The hierarchy of the Archai may be said to do its creating on the human form in rhythmical epochs. At one time they direct the thoughts, whereby the will of each is governed, more toward the extraterrestrial cosmos. Another time they direct them toward the earth. The human form is built by the cooperative activity stimulated by these extraterrestrial cosmic and earthly forces— that form so expressive of the fact that man is both an earthly and an extraterrestrial cosmic being.

The human form described here as the creation of the hierarchy of the Archai comprises more than just the external outline of man and his surfaces as reflected in the boundary of his skin. It includes the organism of forces underlying his bearing, his capacity to move in adjustment to earthly conditions, and his ability to use his body as a medium for the expression of his inner life.

Man owes to the work done on him by the Archai the fact that he can relate in upright posture to the forces of gravity, that by maintaining his balance he can move freely in the gravitational sphere, and that he can overcome gravity in the free movement of his hands and arms. All this and even more that is part of his inner being but still the product of his forming, he owes to the Archai. The groundwork for all of this is laid down in the life that, even in the case of this early period, we may refer to as the life between death and being born again. It is laid down in such a way that in the third, present-day period, man is himself able to work on this forming of his coming life on earth during his life between death and rebirth.

*

GUIDELINES

1. The lives lived between death and rebirth also fall into three successive epochs. In the first, man lives entirely within the hierarchy of the Archai, who prepare his later human form for physical earthly life.

2. The Archai thus prepare man for the later development of free self-consciousness. This can evolve only in the case of beings who are able, out of the inner impulse of their souls, to use the form thus created to bring that self-awareness to expression.

3. We see here how the germinal powers of humanity's qualities and forces that are making their appearance in our present world era were prepared for in long-past cosmic epochs, and how the microcosm issued from the macrocosm.

XVIII

SECOND PART OF THE CONTEMPLATION:
WHAT IS REVEALED WHEN WE LOOK BACK
INTO PAST LIVES BETWEEN DEATH AND REBIRTH?

In a second period, man passes from the realm of the Archai to that of the Archangels. His connection with them, however, is not as bodily-spiritual as it was with the Archai, his relationship to the Archangelic hierarchy is more spiritual. Nevertheless, it is so intimate that we cannot speak of man's being detached as yet from the divine-spiritual world during this period.

The hierarchy of the Archangels bestows on man's etheric body what corresponds on this level to the element of form given him for his physical body by the Archai. The etheric body is adapted to extraterrestrial cosmic conditions, just as the physical body was adapted to the earth by its form, so that it might serve there as the bearer of self-consciousness. The earth lives in the physical body, the starry world in the etheric. Man owes to the creative work done on his etheric body by the Archangels the inner forces that enable him, while living on the earth, to wrest his stance, his motion and his gesture free of earth's influence. In his etheric body live forces that stream from every direction out of the cosmos into the earth, just as his form enables earthly forces to live in his physical body. The earthly forces living in this physically manifested form are such as to make it comparatively fixed and finished. An individual's external shape remains fairly set, subject to only minor changes during the course of an incarnation; his capacity for movement tends to harden into habits, and so on. But in the etheric body constant mobility holds sway, reflecting changes occurring in the constellations during his lifetime. The etheric body even changes in accordance with the changes in the heavens of day and night, as well as in accordance with those occurring between birth and death.

This adaptation of the etheric body to the forces operative in the heavens is not in contradiction to the gradual detaching of the starry skies from the divine-spiritual, spoken of in other contemplations. It is true that divine will and divine intelligence did live in the stars in most ancient times. Later on, the stars passed into the realm of the 'calculable.' The gods no longer influenced man through what had become their wrought work. But through the agency of his etheric body man gradually attained his own independent relationship to the stars, just as his physical body related him to the earth's gravity.

In this second period, the hierarchy of the Archangels created the etheric body, with which man joins himself as he descends to be born upon the earth—an etheric body that has taken up into itself the extraterrestrial forces of the cosmos.

His alliance with a particular earthly group of human beings is an essential element bestowed on man by this hierarchy. People are differentiated over the earth. Looking back into this second period, one sees a differentiation of another, more spiritual kind than that of today's races and nationalities. It stems from the fact that the forces of the stars affect the various regions of the earth differently according to the constellations involved. The starry heavens are mirrored in the life of the earth in such matters as land and water distribution, climate, vegetation, and so on. To the degree that man must adapt himself to *these* conditions, which are actually cosmic conditions obtaining in the earthly sphere, he adjusts to them with his etheric body, and its form is a creation of the choir of the Archangels.

But it is just during this second period that the Luciferic and Ahrimanic powers enter in a special way into human life. This intrusion is a necessary one, even though it would seem at first to drag man *down* below his proper level.

If man is to develop self-awareness in his life on earth, he has to loosen himself to a greater degree from the spiritual world from which he issued than *that* world itself can bring to pass. This occurred in the period when the Archangels were at work on him because his connection with the spiritual world at that time was no longer as firm as it was when he was under the aegis of the Archai. Lucifer and Ahriman are more of a match for the spiritual powers emanating from the Archangels than for the stronger forces of the Archai.

The Luciferic powers impregnate the etheric form with a stronger leaning toward the starry world than it would have if the divine-spiritual beings of man's origin were the only ones to influence him, and the Ahrimanic forces enmesh the physical form more completely in earth's gravity than would be the case if they could not exert their influence.

The seed of full self-consciousness and of free will was thus implanted in the human race. In spite of the fact that the Ahrimanic powers abhor free will, they brought it into embryonic being *in man's nature* by tearing him loose from the divine-spiritual world *of his belonging.*

It was in this second period that what the various hierarchies, from the Seraphim down to the Archangels, have achieved in man was more deeply impressed into the physical and etheric bodies than could have happened without the Luciferic and Ahrimanic influences. If it had not been for those influences, the effect of the work of the hierarchies would have been more on the astral body and the ego.

This was the reason why that more spiritual grouping of humanity striven for by the Archangels, did not take place.

As a result of man's being so deeply impressed into his physical and etheric bodies, the spiritual forces were changed into their opposite. A differentiation into races and nationalities took the place of the more spiritual one that was intended.

Had it not been for the Luciferic and Ahrimanic influences, earthly humanity would have regarded its differentiations as of heavenly origin. The various groupings would have related their lives to one another as beings of a free and loving give and take. Earthly gravity makes a bodily appearance in man in the form of races and nationalities, whereas the divine-spiritual world would have been reflected in a spiritual grouping.

The later achievement in man's evolution of full self-awareness had to be based on these prerequisites. That, in turn, required that the primeval differentiations in existence, at the time when man passed from the aegis of the Exusiai to that of the Archai, remained in a certain, although slightly weakened, form.

Man, feeling and contemplating, experienced this stage of his evolution as though in a cosmic school. He had not as yet come to realize that this was essential preparation for his later self-awareness. But the feeling contemplation of the forces involved in his development was nevertheless important for the membering of self-consciousness into his astral body and his ego.

In regard to thinking, the following occurred at that time. Through the agency of the Luciferic forces, man was endowed with the inclination to continue to immerse himself in early forms of spirituality, not to adapt himself to its newer forms, since Lucifer always strives to preserve earlier forms of life for man's experiencing.

That was the cause of man's thinking taking on a form such that, in his life between death and rebirth, he gradually developed the capacity that had been the shaper of his thoughts in primeval times. At that time, this capacity included spiritual vision, although this scarcely differed from the mere sensory impressions of the present day. At that time, the physical wore the spiritual on its surface. But now the thinking capacity preserved from that period can function only as sensory perception. The capacity to lift oneself to the spiritual in one's thinking gradually declined. This became fully evident for the first time when, in the age of the consciousness soul, the spiritual world became enveloped in total darkness for man's experience. The result was that, in the nineteenth century, the better scientists, unwilling to become materialists, said, "All that remains to us is simply to depend on our senses and explore the world in its aspects of measure, weight and number. But we are not justified in denying the existence of a spiritual world hidden behind the sensory world." This was an admission that there could be an unknown world of light where they were staring only into darkness.

Just as Lucifer distorted thinking, Ahriman distorted will, endowing it with a kind of freedom that should only have come later. This is not freedom in its real aspect, but rather the illusion of it. Humanity lived for a long time in this illusion, so that there was no possibility of developing a spiritually adequate concept of freedom. People argued back and forth over whether man was free or caught in the toils of harsh necessity. When true freedom emerged with the dawning of the age of consciousness, it went unrecognized, so long had the understanding of it been subject to an illusion.

Everything that had impressed itself on man's inner being in this second phase of development between death and rebirth was carried by him as cosmic memory into the third phase, that in which he is still living. In this period, his relationship to the hierarchy of Angels is similar to the relationship he had to the Archangels during the second phase, with the difference that he attains through the Angels to fully independent individuality. They limit their function to bringing about the right relationship between the lives lived between death and rebirth and the lives lived on earth, and this now, not as a choir, but in the relationship of one to one.

A noteworthy fact is that the entire hierarchy of Archangels works on the single human being during the second phase of the evolution of his lives between death and rebirth, whereas, later, the guidance of the nations falls to the lot of this hierarchy. Here, a single Archangel serves as folk spirit for one nationality. The Archai are active on behalf of races and, here again, one being from the hierarchy of the Archai serves one race as its racial spirit.

So present-day man retains the cosmic memory of earlier

phases of after death experience in his present after-life as well. This cosmic memory is clearly present where spiritual guidance is evident in the physical world as, for example, in races and nationalities.

*

GUIDELINES

1. In the second phase of the evolution of lives between death and rebirth, man enters the realm of the Archangels. The seed of his later self-consciousness is implanted during this phase, the predisposition to it in the form of his human figure having been laid down in the first phase.

2. During this second period, Luciferic and Ahrimanic influences thrust man more deeply into the physical than would have been the case without them.

3. In the third period, man enters the realm of the hierarchy of Angels, but they extend their influence only to the astral body and the ego. This period is that in which we are now living. What took place in the first two periods lives on in the evolution of mankind and explains why man of the consciousness-soul age, in the nineteenth century, stares into the spiritual world as into total darkness.

XIX
WHAT IS THE EARTH IN REALITY IN THE MACROCOSMOS?

In the foregoing studies we have looked from the most varied angles at the evolutionary stages of the cosmos and humanity, and have seen how man derives his forces from the extraterrestrial universe, the single exception being those forces from which he obtains his self-awareness. These are given him by the earth.

This statement sums up the significance of the earthly for the human race. But it must be followed by others, answering the question, "What is the earth's significance for the macrocosm?"

We must glance back at what has already been covered if we are to find the answer to this question.

Clairvoyant vision discovers the macrocosm to be the more overflowing with life the further back it looks into the past. In the far past it was so alive that all possibility of measuring any of its vital manifestations ceases. Then man is separated from this livingness. The macrocosm comes increasingly into the realm of the calculable.

But this means it gradually dies. The macrocosm dies to the degree that man, the microcosm, emerges from it as an independent being.

An extinct macrocosm confronts us in the cosmic present. But man is not the only product of its evolution; the earth, too, was born of the macrocosm.

Man, deriving from earth the forces upon which his self-consciousness is founded, is in far too close a relationship to it to have an adequate grasp of its nature and being. As his self-consciousness came into full flowering in the consciousness-soul era, he became accustomed to taking into account only the spatial extension of the universe and to regarding the earth as an insignificant grain of dust in comparison with the physical dimensions of universal space.

It will seem strange, therefore, to hear what spiritual vision has to say about the true significance of this supposed 'grain of dust.'

The earth consists of a mineral foundation in which the plant and animal kingdoms are embedded.

The forces that we see at work in all of their various manifestations as the year runs its course live in these kingdoms. Let us observe the vegetable kingdom. Forces moving toward physical death are to be seen there during autumn and winter. Clairvoyant consciousness becomes aware in this phenomenon of the nature of the forces that have brought the macrocosm to extinction. In spring and summer we see forces of growth and burgeoning at work in plant life. Clairvoyant consciousness sees in these processes not only the source of vegetative abundance for the year in question, but a superabundance, a surplus. This surplus is one of seed potential. Plants are the repositories of more seed forces than they need for the growth of leaves, fruit and blossoms, and for the consciousness that beholds it, this excess of seed potential streams out into the extraterrestrial macrocosm.

Surplus stores of energy ray out similarly into the macrocosm from the mineral kingdom. This energy has the task of bringing the forces issuing from vegetation to their right locations in the macrocosm. Under the influence of the mineral forces, a new model of the macrocosm grows out of the forces of the plant world.

There are also forces issuing similarly from the animal kingdom. But their activity is not like that of the mineral and plant realms in the sense of radiating outward from the earth. Rather do these forces encompass and bring into spherical form everything that has issued from the plant kingdom and been carried out into the universe by the mineral forces to take shape there, with the result that the model of a self-enclosed macrocosm comes into being.

This is the way a consciousness illumined by spiritual insight sees the nature of the terrestrial; that is, as a revivifying element within the extinct macrocosm.

A new macrocosm will develop from this 'grain of dust' earth as the old, extinct one falls into dissolution, just as the whole large plant grows up out of a spatially insignificant seed after the old plant has fallen into decay.

To see the earth as everywhere a world in germination is to see it truly.

Man carries on his existence on the earth in the midst of this germinating life, taking part in the germinating as well as in the extinct life. He derives his thinking forces from the extinct element. As long as these forces issued from the still living macrocosm of the past, they were not the basis of self-consciousness. They lived as growth forces in a humanity still lacking any consciousness of self. The thinking powers may not possess any life of their own if they are to provide the basis of free human self-awareness. Their role is to be, like the extinct macrocosm, dead shadows of the aliveness of a past cosmic era.

Man participates, on the other hand, in the germinating process of the earth, from which the forces of his will emanate. These will forces are alive, but for just that reason man cannot participate in them with his self-consciousness. Within his being they radiate into the shadows that are his thoughts. They are suffused by these shadows, and man's full, free self-awareness lives its way into him, in the age of the consciousness soul, in that suffusing of the free thought unfolding its life within earth's germinating being.

The past, casting shadows, the future harboring seeds of reality, meet in man's being. Their meeting is the present-day life of man.

That this is how matters stand is at once perceptible to clairvoyant consciousness when it enters the region of the spirit immediately adjoining the physical realm; it is also the region wherein one finds Michael active.

All the earth's life becomes transparent for those who sense how the seed of a new universe underlies it. Every plant form, every stone appears in a new light to the human soul who is aware of how each and every one of these, in its life and in its form, contributes to making the earth as an entity the seed-embryo of a newly sprouting macrocosm.

Let anyone but once try to bring the thoughts of these facts to full life within himself and he will feel what this can signify for the human mind.

*

GUIDELINES

1. At the start of the consciousness-soul age, human beings became accustomed to turn their attention to the physical size of the spatial universe and to consider this in first place. They therefore called the earth a 'grain of dust' in this macrocosm that appeared so vast.

2. This 'grain of dust' reveals itself to clairvoyant consciousness to be the seed foundation of a new macrocosm-to-be, whereas the old one shows itself extinct. The latter had to die out in order that man might sever himself from it in full self-consciousness.

3. In the cosmic present man participates with his liberating thought forces in the extinct macrocosm, whereas, with his will forces, whose nature must remain hidden from him, he participates in the life of the newly germinating macrocosm-to-be, the earth.

XX

SLEEP AND WAKING
IN THE LIGHT OF THE FOREGOING CONTEMPLATION

The theme of sleep and waking has been a frequent focus of anthroposophical study, and we have pursued it from a great variety of angles. But every approach to new aspects of the world's content requires a deepening of the understanding we already have of such basic facts of life. Our discussion of the earth as the seed of a newly evolving macrocosm provides just such opportunities for looking with deepened understanding at sleep and waking.

Human beings live while awake in the thought shadows cast by an extraterrestrial world and in will impulses whose inner nature we can no more penetrate with our ordinary consciousness than we can follow what is taking place in deep, dreamless sleep.

Man's independently functioning self-consciousness is born of the in-streaming into his thought shadows of these subconscious impulses of will. The ego lives in this self-consciousness.

When, in this condition, man experiences the world around him, his inner sensing is permeated by extraterrestrial, cosmic impulses that extend from a remote past into the present. He is not aware of this. A man can be aware of a fact only when he participates in it with those of his forces that are dying, not with those waxing forces that endow him with life. So man experiences himself by losing from sight what lies at the very foundation of his inner being. But this is just why he is able, while awake, to sense himself wholly in his thought shadows. No welling up of life keeps him from participating in what is extinct. But a 'life in the extinct' conceals the true nature of the earthly, namely, that it is the

121

seed of a new universe. In his waking life, man does not see the earth as it is. The fact of its beginning cosmic life escapes him.

Such is man's life in what the earth gives him as the basis of his self-awareness. In the era of his self-conscious ego development, he loses from sight the true picture of his inner impulses as well as of his environment. But it is in this floating above the world's reality that he experiences the reality of his ego and feels himself to be a self-conscious being. Above him, the extraterrestrial cosmos; beneath him, an earthly world, the nature of which remains hidden from him; between the two, the manifestations of his free ego, its real being radiant with the full brightness of knowledge and free will.

How different is the state of sleeping! In his astral body and his ego, man shares the earth's germinating life. The most intensive 'will to life' is active in all about him during dreamless sleep. This life permeates his dreams, although not so strongly that he cannot experience them in a kind of semi-consciousness. Perceiving his dreams in this semi-consciousness, man senses the forces whereby the cosmos weaves the fabric of his being. In the flashing up of dreams, the quickening effect of the astral streaming into man's etheric body becomes visible. Thoughts are still alive in this flashing up. It is only upon awakening that they are laid hold of by the forces that bring about their death and reduce them to shadows.

This connection between dream pictures and waking thoughts is a significant one. Man thinks with the same forces that enable him to grow and live, but they must die if he is to become a thinker.

Here is the point at which we can arrive at a proper understanding of why it is that man grasps reality in thought. His thoughts provide him with the dead picture of what has built him up out of the substance of living reality.

A dead picture, yes; but it is the product of the creating of the greatest painter, the cosmos itself. True, life is missing from the picture. But if life were present in it, there could be no ego development. As it is, the picture contains the entire content of the universe in all its glory.

In my *Philosophy of Freedom* I called attention, as fully as the context permitted, to the inner relationship that exists between thinking and the world's reality. This is at the place where I talk of the bridge that leads from the depths of the thinking ego to the depths of the reality of nature.

The reason why sleep blots out perception for ordinary consciousness is that it plunges the sleeper into earth's germinating life as this burgeons out into the newly developing macrocosm. When imaginative consciousness counteracts this extinguishing, the soul perceives, not a sharply contoured earth of mineral, plant and animal kingdoms, but a living process enkindled in the earth and flaming out into the macrocosm.

The situation is this. If man is to arrive at independent self-awareness, he must lift himself, waking, with his own essential ego reality out of the essential reality of the cosmos. Sleeping, he reunites himself with that reality.

That, at the present cosmic moment, is the rhythm of man's earthly existence: the experience of his own being outside the world's 'inwardness,' alternating with his life within that inwardness but with the consciousness of his own being blotted out.

In the state between death and a new birth, man's ego lives within the beings of the spirit world. His consciousness there includes everything that was withheld from it during his waking life on earth. He beholds the panorama of macrocosmic forces from the time of their greatest aliveness in the remote past to their extinct condition in the present age. But he also perceives the earthly forces that are the seed of the evolving macrocosm. Furthermore, he looks there into the periods of his sleep exactly as, during his life on earth, he saw earth shining in the sunlight.

It is due solely to the fact that the macrocosm as we know it today has become extinct that, in his life between death and rebirth, man is able to lead a life characterized by a higher degree of awakeness than that of his waking life on earth—an awakeness that makes it possible for him fully to master those forces perceived in the swift, flickering passage of his dreams. These forces fill up the entire cosmos; they are all-pervading. Man receives from them the impulses out of which he shapes that great macrocosmic work of art, his body, as he makes his gradual descent to earth.

What, in our dreams, is a sun-bereft glimmering lives in the spirit world spirit-sun-suffused, waiting to be called upon by the beings of the higher hierarchies or by man for the creative shaping of new life.

*

GUIDELINES

1. If man is to achieve full, independent self-consciousness in his waking state, he has to forego experience of the true shape of reality, both in his own existence and in that of nature. He lifts himself out of the sea of this reality in order, in the shadow nature of his thoughts, to make his own ego his own real experience.

2. During his sleep, man lives with the life of the earth's environment, but that life blots out his self-awareness.

3. The powerful life of cosmic reality out of which man's being is woven and from which he builds his body as he makes his descent from the spirit world flickers up in the semi-consciousness of dreaming. During the period of his life on earth, this powerful life of cosmic reality in him is reduced, in the thought shadows, to the point of extinction. Only in that dead condition can it serve as the basis of man's self-awareness.

XXI
GNOSIS AND ANTHROPOSOPHY

At the time of the consummation of the Mystery of Golgotha, 'Gnosis' was the way of thinking of that section of humanity able to approach this weightiest event in earthly evolution with understanding born, not just of feeling, but of insight.

To understand the state of mind that prevailed when Gnosis lived in human souls, we must realize that the age in which it flourished was that in which the intellectual soul was developing. This fact serves to explain as well the almost total disappearance of Gnosis from the scene of history, a disappearance that, if it is not understood, must remain one of the most puzzling incidents ever to occur in the evolution of the human race.

The development of the intellectual soul was preceded by that of the sentient soul, and this was preceded in its turn by the development of the sentient body. When the facts of the world were perceived by the sentient body, all knowledge was a matter of living in the senses. The world was perceived as sounding, colorful, and so on. But it was recognized that a world of spiritual beings was present in the tones and colors and warmth. There was no talk of 'matter' being the seat of colors, warmth, etc., but rather of spiritual beings manifest in what the senses perceived.

In that age there was as yet no special development of mind coincident with human sensory perception. A person either gave himself wholly to the world about him, in which case the gods revealed themselves to him through his senses, or else he withdrew from the outer world and felt a dim life going on within him.

A significant change occurred when the sentient soul embarked on its development. Revelations of the divine through sensory perception faded away, and in their place came sense impressions issuing from a more or less god-abandoned scene of colors, warmth states, and so on. The divine manifested itself in a spiritual form, as pictorial ideas, to man's awareness. Henceforth, man perceived the world in a two-fold way: externally through his sense impressions, and inwardly through spiritual impressions coming to him as ideas.

Man now had to develop the ability to perceive these inner, spiritual impressions in just as definite a form as that in which he received his previous sense impressions of a god-permeated world. He was able to do this during the era of the sentient soul because his pictorial ideas rose from within him in full definition. He was filled from within by a sense-free spiritual content which was an image of the world content. Where, earlier, the gods had revealed themselves to him clad in sensory form, they now showed themselves to him in spiritual guise.

That is the period in which Gnosis came into being and flourished. It lived as wonderful knowledge in which those men who developed their inner being in purity, participated in such a way that the content of the divine world could be revealed through it. From the fourth to the first millenium before the Mystery of Golgotha, Gnosis was the path of knowledge of the most advanced portion of the human race.

Thereafter, the age of the intellectual soul set in. Pictorial experience of the gods no longer emerged of itself in the inner man. Inner soul effort was essential to evoking it from the human soul. The external world with its sense impressions became a question to which answers were found by summoning up inner strength to evoke images of the divine world.

But these images were pale compared to what they had been previously. This was the state of soul that developed so wondrously among the Greeks. The native of Greece felt himself to be living in an external world of sense impressions, and he was sensitive to its magical influence, which stimulated his inner capacity to evoke the cosmic pictures. Platonism was the philosophical reflection of this soul state.

But the world of the mysteries stood in the background of all of this. It faithfully preserved what remained of Gnosis from the sentient-soul age. Human souls were trained there for this work of preservation. The intellectual soul developed in the course of ordinary evolution, but the sentient soul was brought through schooling to a special enlivening. So it was just in the intellectual-soul period that a rich development of the mysteries went on behind ordinary cultural life.

Divine world images also continued to live within the mysteries to the extent that they were made the content of ritual there. If one looks into the inner aspect of these mysteries, one finds the world pictured there in the most marvellous ritualistic ceremonies.

The human beings who had this experience were the same individuals who, at the time of its consummation, understood the Mystery of Golgotha in its profound cosmic context. But this life of the mysteries held itself aloof from any contact with the world's ordinary concerns, in order to insure a pure development of the divine picture world, a development that became increasingly difficult for the human soul.

In the highest mystery centers, divine beings descended from the spiritual world to support the efforts of human beings struggling for insight. In this way the impulses of the sentient-soul age continued to develop under the influence of the gods themselves. A form of Mystery-Gnosis, known only to a rare few, came into being. Alongside it there existed what people were able to absorb of it with the powers of the intellectual soul. Such was the exoteric form of Gnosis, fragments of which have come down to later times.

In the esoteric Gnosis of the mysteries, people grew ever less capable of lifting themselves to sentient-soul development. Esoteric wisdom degenerated increasingly into a mere concern with the 'gods.' This is one of the secrets of mankind's historical evolution that 'divine mysteries' were at work in it from the first Christian centuries until well into the Middle Ages.

In these 'divine mysteries,' angel beings preserved for earthly life what human beings were no longer able to preserve. Mystery-Gnosis thus kept on living, while exoteric Gnosis was being systematically exterminated.

This treasure of world images, which spiritual beings preserved by spiritual means in Mystery-Gnosis as long as its influence was needed to further the evolution of the human race, could not be retained for man's conscious understanding. But its content of feeling was to be retained and given at the right cosmic moment to a humanity ready for it, in order that the consciousness soul, clothed in its soul warmth might find it possible, later on, to penetrate in a new way into the realm of the spirit. Spiritual beings thus built a bridge from the old world content to the new.

Indications of this secret of human evolution exist. The holy jasper chalice of the Grail from which Christ drank when he broke bread, the vessel in which Joseph of Arimathea caught the blood from Jesus's wounds and in which, therefore, the secret of Golgotha was preserved, was taken over—as legend has it—by the angels awaiting the moment when the castle of the Grail was built by Titurel and they could let the cup descend to those prepared to receive it.

Spiritual beings preserved the world images in which the secrets of Golgotha lived. When the right moment came, they sent down into human souls not the picture content, for that was not possible, but the feeling content.

This implanting of the legacy of feeling inherited from an ancient path of knowledge could serve only as a stimulus, but as a most powerful one, toward the development in our time of a new and full understanding of the Mystery of Golgotha born of the consciousness soul and illumined by the activity of Michael.

Anthroposophy seeks to attain to this new understanding. We can see from the above that it cannot be a renewal of Gnosis, which derived its content from traveling the path of knowledge attuned to the sentient soul, but must instead rely on a totally new method to derive an equally rich content from the consciousness soul.

*

GUIDELINES

1. Gnosis developed in its true form in the age of the sentient soul (the fourth to first millenium before the consummation of the Mystery of Golgotha). In this period, the 'divine' revealed itself to man as inner spiritual content in contrast to its revelation in the previous, sentient-body era in the form of sense impressions of the outer world.

2. In the age of the intellectual soul, this divine-spiritual content could be experienced only in a diminished form. Gnosis was preserved in strictly guarded mysteries. Since it was no longer possible for human beings to do so, due to their inability to revivify the sentient soul, spiritual beings carried over into the Middle Ages, not indeed a content of knowledge, but one of feelings. (The legend of the Grail contains hints of these facts.) While this was happening, exoteric Gnosis, with its appeal to the intellectual soul, was being exterminated.

3. Anthroposophy cannot be a renewal of Gnosis, for that depended on the sentient soul stage of development. Anthroposophy must instead work in Michael's light to achieve an understanding of Christ and of the world in a new way, out of the powers of the consciousness soul. Gnosis was a way of knowledge preserved from earlier times, but the one best suited, at the time of the occurrence of the Mystery of Golgotha, to convey its meaning to human understanding.

XXII

HUMAN FREEDOM AND THE AGE OF MICHAEL

There lives in the human faculty of memory a personalized reproduction of a cosmic force that has been working on man's being in the way described in our recent contemplations. But this cosmic force is still at work. It confers the power to grow, and is the enlivening impulse underlying human life. These are its main functions. But it reserves a small part of its strength for use in consciousness-soul activity, and there it works as the ability to remember.

We must look at this ability in the proper light.

When, in the present epoch of human evolution, man is perceiving with his senses, this perception is a momentary flashing up in his consciousness of pictures of the world. This flashing up occurs as he trains a sense organ on the world around him. It lights up his consciousness, and then disappears again as he ceases to train that sense on the outer world.

This flashing up in the human soul is not allowed to last because, if man were unable to obliterate it promptly from his consciousness, he would lose himself to its picture content; he would no longer be himself. Such a lighting up in his consciousness, as the result of perceiving, is permitted only short duration in the form of so-called after-images which were of such interest to Goethe. Furthermore, this content of consciousness is not allowed to become fixed as essential being; it must remain pictorial in nature. It must not become real, any more than the reflections in a mirror can become real. Man would lose himself just as much to anything that attained reality in his consciousness as he would to anything possessing permanence in its own nature. Here, too, he could no longer be himself.

Sensory perceptions of the surrounding world are thus acts of inner painting on the part of the human soul, a painting without pigments, a painting in spiritual comings-into-being and spiritual passings-away. Like the rainbow that comes into being in nature and then fades away again, leaving not a trace, perceptions come and go without being able of themselves to leave any imprint on memory.

But with every perception another process goes on between man's soul and the outer world. It is a process that takes place in deeper lying levels of his soul life, where growth forces and life impulses are at work. In *this* portion of the soul's life, perception results in more than the production of a fleeting picture; it leaves a real and lasting imprint. Man can endure this because it is real world content which plays a part in his own existence. Its production no more causes him to lose himself than does his growing and digesting, which he carries on without full consciousness.

Memories summoned up from within an individual are inner perceptions of what was left by the second process that takes place in external perceiving.

Again the soul paints, but now its pictures are of the past living on within an individual's own inner being. Again no lasting reality is allowed to take shape in the painting consciousness, but merely an image that comes into being and then disappears again.

Such is the connection between the perceiving of mental images and remembering in the human soul.

But the forces of memory are constantly trying to become more than they can be if man is not to lose himself as a self-conscious being. These forces are remnants of past phases of human evolution, and fall as such under Lucifer's dominion. Lucifer's striving is so to condense impressions of the outer world within man's being that they keep on shining in his consciousness as mental pictures. This striving would be crowned with success if it were not opposed by the Michaelic forces, which do not allow these paintings in inner light to become fixed as reality but maintain the flux of their coming and going as mere pictures.

But the surplus energy surging forth from man's inner being under Lucifer's influence will be transformed in the age of Michael into the power to imagine, for imaginative energy will gradually penetrate into the prevailing intellectual consciousness of the human race. Man, however, will not burden his present-day consciousness with lasting reality that remains active in the constant flow of appearing and disappearing pictures. But he reaches into a higher spiritual world with his imaginations, just as, conversely, he reaches into his own being with his memories. He does not retain these imaginations within him; they are embodied in cosmic existence from which he can always reproduce them in the picturings of his conceptual life.

What Michael saves from fixity in man's inner being is thus taken over by the spiritual world; what man experiences of the power of conscious imagining becomes at the same time world content. It is due to the Mystery of Golgotha that this is possible. The Christ force, which is united with the earth, imprints man's imagination on the cosmos. So long as this force was not yet bound up with the earth, but worked instead from outside it as the sun force, all impulses of growth and life went into man's inner being. They built and maintained him from the cosmos. Since the Christ impulse entered the life of the earth, man was given back to the cosmos with his self-conscious being.

Man has developed from a cosmic being into a being of the earth. He has been predestined to become again a cosmic being after having become himself as an earthly being.

The possibility of developing freedom is due to the fact that in his momentary conceptualizing man lives, not in reality itself, but only in a reflection of it, in a pictorial life. All reality in consciousness compels. Pictures cannot compel, however. If something happens as the product of an impression made by a picture, it happens independently of the picture itself. Man becomes free in that he lifts himself with his consciousness soul out of the realm of real existence to emerge in the non-reality of pictorial experiencing.

So the significant question arises: Does an individual not lose essential being when he deserts it with part of himself and plunges into non-being? This is again a point at which, in our study of the world, we confront a great riddle.

The mental images experienced in our consciousness originate in the cosmos. It is in relation to the cosmos that man plunges into non-being. In his forming of mental images he frees himself from all cosmic influences. He paints the cosmos as an outsider to it.

If that were the whole story, freedom would light up in a person for a cosmic moment, but in that same moment his human reality would dissolve. But although he becomes liberated from the cosmos in forming mental images, he is nevertheless connected in his subconscious soul life to his previous incarnations and to the lives he has lived between death and rebirth. In his conscious life he lives in a pictorial state of being though maintaining himself with his subconsciousness in spiritual reality. While his present ego is experiencing freedom, his ego of the past keeps him within the realm of real being.

With respect to that real being, a person engaged in forming mental images is wholly given over to what he has become as a result of his cosmic and terrestrial past.

Human evolution shows us at this point in its panorama the abyss of nothingness over which man leaps in becoming a free being. Michaelic activity and the Christ impulse make this leap possible.

*

GUIDELINES

1. In forming mental images, man lives with his consciousness soul, not in real being, but in the non-reality of

134

the picture state. This frees him from participating in the cosmic. Pictures do not compel; only real being has the power to do so. If man nevertheless acts in accordance with his picturing, it is done quite independently of the pictures. Hence, he is acting in freedom from the world.

2. At the moment of forming such mental images, man is connected with the world's essential being only through what he has become as a result of his past lives on earth and in the spiritual world between death and rebirth.

3. Man is able to make the leap over the abyss of non-being, where the cosmos is concerned, only because of Michael's activity and the Christ impulse.

XXIII

WHERE IS MAN
AS A THINKING AND REMEMBERING BEING?

In his forming of mental images (thinking) and his experiencing of memories, man finds himself in the sphere of the physical world. But no matter in what direction he looks, his senses will never discover anything there that could supply him with the forces essential to pictorial conceiving or to remembering.

Self-consciousness appears on the scene in the formation of mental images. In the sense of our previous studies, this is the product of terrestrial forces. But the forces in question are of a type inaccessible to sensory perception. While man is on earth, he does indeed develop thoughts based solely on what his senses convey. But the power to think gives him nothing of the content of his thoughts.

Where do we find this force that forms mental images (thoughts) and memory pictures out of the terrestrial?

We discover it when we look in spirit at what man brings with him from previous earthly lives. Our ordinary consciousness knows nothing of this because it exists at a subconscious level. But when man returns to the earth after his sojourn in the spirit, it immediately betrays its relationship to those earthly forces that do not belong in the realm of sensory observation and sensory thinking.

Man is not of this realm with respect to the forming of mental images (thinking), but rather with his will activity, which runs the course destiny prescribes.

Considering the fact that the earth harbors forces lying outside the sensory realm, we can speak of 'spiritual earth' as the counterpart of the physical. It then follows that man as a will being lives in and with the spiritual earth, but that as an

137

image forming (thinking) being he lives within the physical earthly sphere, but not, as a thinking being, with it.

As a thinking being, man brings forces of the spiritual world into the physical, but he remains with these forces a spiritual being who merely appears in the physical world without entering into any community with it.

During his lifetime on the earth, the image forming (thinking) human being enters into community with the 'spiritual earth' only. His self-awareness grows out of this communion. It therefore owes its existence to those processes of a spiritual nature in which man is involved during the course of his earthly lifetime.

If one looks spiritually at the full panorama of what has been described here, one beholds the 'human ego' in perspective.

Where experiences involving memory are concerned, one enters the area of the astral body. In the process of remembering, not only do the results of previous earthly lives stream into the ego of the present moment, as they do in the case of image forming (thinking), but the forces of the spiritual world experienced by man between death and rebirth stream into his inner being. It is the astral body into which they stream.

Now there exists within the physical earth no area into which these instreaming forces can be directly received. Man is just as incapable of connecting himself, as a remembering being, with the things and processes perceived by his senses as he is when he forms mental images. But he does enter into community with the element that, although not itself of a physical nature, nevertheless transforms the physical into dynamic processes and happenings. This is the element of rhythm found in processes in nature and in human life. There is in nature rhythmical interchange between day and night, and between the seasons. Breathing and the circulation of the blood are rhythmical processes in man, as is also the rhythm between sleeping and waking, and so on.

Neither in nature nor in man are rhythmical processes physical. They could be called semi-spiritual. The physical as object is lost sight of in the rhythmical process. In the act of remembering, man's being is transposed into his own and nature's rhythm. He lives in his astral body.

The goal of Indian yoga is to enter wholly into the experience of rhythm. It turns its back on the ego realm of image forming and, in an inner experience similar to remembering, contemplates the world lying behind that accessible to ordinary consciousness.

It is not proper for the spiritual life of the West to suppress the ego in pursuit of knowledge. The western task is rather to educate the ego to perceive the spirit.

This cannot be achieved by progressing from the sensory world into the world of rhythm in such a manner as to experience in rhythm merely the translation of the physical into the semi-spiritual. Rather must that region of the spiritual world be sought out that reveals itself in the rhythmic element.

Hence, two possibilities exist. First, an experiencing of the physical in the rhythmical in the sense of the physical becoming semi-spiritual. This is an earlier path no longer suited to the present. Second, an experiencing of the spiritual world whose sphere is the realm of universal rhythm in and outside man, just as man's sphere is the earthly world with its physical occupants and processes.

Now, everything that happens in the present cosmic moment as a result of Michael's activity belongs in this sphere. In that he makes the world of rhythm his dwelling place, a spiritual being of Michael's nature brings everything that would otherwise be part of Lucifer's domain into the realm of purely human development, which is not subject to Luciferic influence.

All this can be viewed by individuals who approach it with imaginative vision. In the exercise of imagination the soul lives in rhythm, and Michael's sphere is the world that reveals itself in rhythm.

Memory, too, is at home in that world, but it does not enter it deeply. Ordinary consciousness has no experience of it. But for one who exercises imagination, the world of subjective memories rises to the surface out of the world of rhythm. But these memories are immediately absorbed into the archetypal forms of the physical that were created by the divine-spiritual and live in the realm of the etheric. One experiences the etheric as it flashes up in cosmic images and harbors world creating powers within itself. The sun forces weaving in this ether do not merely radiate light; they conjure forth from it prototypal pictures of the world-to-be. The sun is seen to be the cosmic painter of the universe. It is the cosmic counterpart of the impulses that, in man, paint the mental images of his thinking process.

*

GUIDELINES

1. Although man as a thinking being lives in the physical earthly realm, he does not enter into any sort of community with it. In his life as a spiritual being he perceives the physical realm, but he obtains his thinking forces from the 'spiritual earth' in the same way that he comes to the experience of his destiny as the outcome of his previous incarnations.

2. The content of memory is experienced in the sphere wherein the physical becomes semi-spiritual in rhythm and wherein such spiritual processes take place as those resulting at the present cosmic moment from the activity of Michael.

3. A person who really arrives at an understanding of thinking and memory comes to grasp how man as a being of the earth, living with the earthly sphere, refrains from entering fully into it, and strives instead, with his extraterrestrial being, toward self-consciousness as the perfecting of the ego through community with the 'spiritual earth.'

XXIV
MAN IN HIS MACROCOSMIC BEING

The cosmos reveals itself to man in the first instance from an earthly aspect and from the extraterrestrial aspect of the world of the stars.

Man feels related to the earth and its forces. Life instructs him unmistakably about this relationship.

He does not at present sense himself equally related to the starry world, but this lasts only as long as he remains unconscious of his etheric body. To take hold of the etheric body in imaginations is to develop a feeling of kinship with the world of the stars in the same way that consciousness of the physical body conveys a sense of belonging to the earth.

The forces that put the etheric body in the world come from the periphery of the cosmos, whereas the forces of the physical body ray out from the center of the earth.

But the etheric forces streaming into the earth from the cosmic environment are accompanied by the cosmic impulses active in man's astral body. The ether is like an ocean in which astral forces swim toward the earth from every part of universal space.

In the present cosmic era, only the mineral and plant kingdoms are able to enter into a direct relationship with the astrality streaming into the earth on the waves of the ether. The animal and human kingdoms cannot do this.

In the case of the animal kingdom, spiritual vision shows that what lives in the embryo is not the astrality presently streaming into the earthly sphere, but rather the astrality of the ancient moon period.

In the case of the plant kingdom, one sees how its great variety of wondrous forms are given shape by the astral separating from the ether and extending its activity over the plant world.

With the animal world, one sees how an astral element, active in an earlier epoch during the evolution of the moon, has been kept active by spiritual forces; it remains presently in the spiritual world, continuing to be active as in its earlier function, and does not enter the etheric sphere.

The influence of this astral element is also mediated by those moon forces that have likewise continued their activity from the previous earthly stage.

In the animal kingdom, then, we have the product of impulses that manifested themselves in external nature in the foregoing earthly phase, whereas in the present cosmic era they have withdrawn into the spiritual world that is actively streaming through the earth.

Now, spiritual observation finds that in the animal kingdom only those astral forces of an earlier time that are preserved in present-day earthly conditions are of significance for the permeation of the physical and etheric bodies by the astral body. But once the animal has its astral body, sun impulses become active in it. Though sun forces cannot confer the astral element on animal nature, once the animal possesses that element, sun forces are charged with providing for its growth and nutrition, and so forth.

The situation is a different one for man. He, too, receives his astrality from the old, preserved moon forces. The sun forces, however, harbor astral impulses that, while remaining without effect on the animal kingdom, go on working in man's astrality in continuation of the work done on it by the forces of the moon when the latter first permeated man with the astral element.

The moon world can be perceived in the astral body of the animal, whereas we perceive in the human astral body the harmonious working together of both the sun and moon worlds.

It is due to this sun-like element in man's astral body that he can absorb the spiritual radiating in the earthly sphere and use it in the building up of his self-consciousness. The astral element streams in from the periphery of the cosmos, working either as a contemporary force or as a hold-over from an earlier time. But everything related to the shaping of the ego as the bearer of self-consciousness has to ray out from a stellar center. The astral works from the circumference, while what is related to the ego works from a central point. Earth-as-star transmits its impulse to the human ego from its center. Every star radiates from its center forces whereby the ego of some being or other receives its shaping.

Here we see a demonstration of the polarity of star center and cosmic periphery.

It also enables us to see how the animal kingdom is still present as a product of earlier evolutionary forces of the being earth, how it is using up the astral forces that have been held over, but how it will have to disappear when the latter are used up. In man's case, conversely, fresh astral forces are being garnered from the sun sphere, forces that enable him to continue his development into the future.

It becomes evident from the above that man's nature cannot be understood unless one is as aware of stellar reality as one is of his connection with the earth.

What man receives from the earth for the development of his self-awareness is also a gift of the spiritual world active within the earthly realm. The fact that the sun sphere gives man what he needs for his astrality is attributable to activity that went on during the ancient sun phase. It was during that phase that the earth received the capacity to develop mankind's ego impulses. The spiritual element of that period is what the earth has preserved for itself from that sun element, but it must be kept from dying out by the sun activity of the present.

The earth itself was once the sun. Then it passed into a spiritualized state. In the present phase of cosmic development the sun is active from without, and this activity constantly rejuvenates the senescent spiritual element of an earlier phase. This sun element active in the present also protects that of the earlier phase from falling victim to Lucifer, since anything that continues its activity without being absorbed into the forces of the present day becomes Lucifer's prey.

In this cosmic epoch, man's sense of belonging to the world beyond the earth can be said to be so dim that he is not consciously aware of it. It is not only dim; it is drowned out by his sense of kinship with the earthly. Since man must find his self-awareness in the earthly realm, he grows so strongly united with it during the early part of the consciousness-soul age that it has a stronger effect on him than is consonant with the right development of his soul life. Man is, so to speak, bedazzled by impressions of the sensory world and, in that overwhelmed condition, he fails to rise to a thinking process that is inwardly alive and independent.

This whole period, from the middle of the nineteenth century on, has been one in which people have been bedazzled by sensory impressions. The great illusion of the period has been that the overpowering life of the senses, which strives to blot out life in the extraterrestrial cosmos, is the right one.

The Ahrimanic powers were able to do as they wanted with people in this state of bedazzlement. Lucifer was more restrained by the sun's influence than Ahriman, who was in a position to nurture, particularly in men of science, the dangerous notion that ideas are applicable to sensory impressions only. That is why Anthroposophy meets with little understanding in scientific circles. People confront the findings of spiritual science and try to grasp them conceptually, but their ideas cannot comprehend spiritual matters because their inner experiencing is overwhelmed by an Ahrimanic approach to knowledge based on the senses. This makes them fear falling into blind dependence on authority if they give any heed to what the spiritual observer has to report.

So, in the second half of the nineteenth century, the world beyond the earth grew ever darker for human consciousness. If man regains the capacity to experience ideas even when they are not based on the support of the senses, seekers will again find light streaming toward them from the extraterrestrial universe, and this will mean coming to know Michael in his realm.

When the time comes in which people celebrate the autumnal festival of Michael with true depth and inwardness, the celebrants will feel developing with utmost clarity in their consciousness this guiding thought: The soul given over to ideas experiences spirit light when sensory appearances echo only as memories in man.

A person who can have this experience will also be able to return from the festival mood to a right relationship with the world of the senses, and Ahriman will not find it possible to harm him.

*

GUIDELINES

1. At the beginning of the consciousness-soul age, a dimming of the sense of belonging to the world beyond the earth took place. On the other hand, a feeling of belonging to the earth in experiencing sensory impressions grew so strong, particularly in scientific circles, that it amounted to a state of bedazzlement.

2. The Ahrimanic powers have an especially dangerous influence in this condition, because people live under the illusion that a bedazzled experience of sensory impressions is good and right and represents a real advance in evolution.

3. Man must develop the strength to illumine his world of ideas and to experience it as light-filled, even in cases where the ideas involved are not based on the bedazzling world of the senses. An awareness of belonging to the cosmic realm beyond the earth will awaken in experiencing the independent and independently illumined world of ideas. The basis for Michaelic festivals will grow out of this feeling.

XXV

MAN'S SENSING AND THINKING ORGANIZATIONS IN THEIR RELATIONSHIP TO THE WORLD

When a person applies imaginative cognition to a study of his own human nature, he eliminates his sensory equipment from the scene before him; he becomes, in his view of himself, a being without a sense organism. He does not stop seeing pictures derived from previous sensory experience, but he ceases to feel them relating him to the external world. The pictures of the physical world that he now confronts are not based on sensory perception. He sees them in spirit, independently of the senses, and they constitute proof that behind his sensory connection with the external world man is related to it in another way also, a way not based on his physical senses. This relationship is to the spirit incarnated in the external world of nature.

In this approach, the physical world drops out of the scene man is contemplating. It is the earthly element that falls away; man no longer feels it to be part of him.

We might believe that this means the disappearance of his self-consciousness. This would seem to be consistent with our previous studies, in which self-consciousness was represented as being the outcome of man's connection with the being of the earth. But the facts are otherwise. Man keeps what he had gained from the earth, even when, after attaining it, he divests himself of the earthly in a living experience of insight.

The spiritually imaginative approach described makes it clear that man has not actually formed a close bond with his sense organism. It is really not he himself but rather the surrounding world that lives in that organism. This world has built itself and its nature into man's sensory equipment.

For this reason, a person exercising imaginative perception looks upon his sense organism as a component of the outer world, a part of it that—though more closely related to him than the world of nature—still remains an external world. It is distinguished from the rest of the outer world only by the fact that man cannot enter that world for purposes of insight except through the agency of his sensory perception, whereas he actually has living experience through his sense organism. This organism is part of the external world, but man projects into it his soul-spiritual being, which he brings with him from the spiritual sphere upon entering into earthly existence. Except for the fact that he permeates this organism with his soul-spiritual being, it is every bit as much outer world as is the plant world extending around him. In the last analysis, the eye belongs to the world, not to man, just as the rose that he perceives belongs to the world rather than to him.

In the epoch of cosmic evolution upon which we have recently embarked, scientists have been saying that color and tone and warmth impressions exist in man himself, not in the world outside him. In reality, the 'color red' is not out there in man's environment, but simply the effect of an unknown element on those who perceive it. But the exact opposite is true. Color does not belong to the human eye. The eye and the color it perceives belong rather to the world. It is not true that during man's lifetime on the earth he allows his terrestrial environment to flow into him; rather is he growing out into that environment between birth and death.

It is significant that the correct view of man's relationship to the world about him was twisted into exactly the opposite picture of the facts at the close of the dark age, when man was staring into the world without glimpsing even a premonitory ray of spiritual light.

Once a person exercising imaginative cognition has stripped away the world he lives in with his sense organization, he begins to have an experience of another organization that supports thinking in the same way that the sense organization supports pictorial sensory perception. Such a person now feels himself to be connected with the surrounding starry universe by this thinking organization, just as he previously felt himself connected with his earthly environment by his sense organization. He comes to know himself as a cosmic being. His thoughts are no longer shadow pictures. They are as much saturated with reality as were the sensory images of his sensory experience.

If he now achieves the further stage of inspiration, he becomes aware that he can lay aside this world supporting the thinking organization in the same way that he stripped off the terrestrial world. He recognizes that in the case of this organization also he belongs not to himself but to the world. He realizes how cosmic thoughts live in him through the agency of his personal thought organization. He again becomes aware that he thinks not by absorbing pictures of the world but by *growing out* with his thought organization into cosmic thinking.

Man is world with respect to both his sense organization and his thinking system. The world builds itself into him. Thus he is world content rather than himself in sensory perception and in thinking.

Into his thought organization, then, man projects his soul-spiritual being, which belongs neither to the earth nor to the starry world, but which is of a wholly spiritual nature and goes on with him from earthly life to earthly life. This soul-spiritual element is accessible to inspiration only.

With this development, man leaves his earthly and cosmic organizations to contemplate himself with inspired cognition as a purely soul-spiritual being. In this aspect he enters the realm ruled by destiny.

Man lives with his sense organization in his physical body, with his thinking organization in the etheric. Upon laying aside these two organizations, he has a living experience of his astral body.

Every time man lays aside a portion of his acquired being, he is the richer for it, although his soul content is impoverished thereby. Although the beauty of the material plant world pales for him when he lays aside his physical body, the whole world of elemental beings that lives in the plant realm appears to his inner contemplation.

For this reason, no one truly knowledgeable in spiritual matters has an ascetic attitude toward what the senses reveal. Throughout his experiencing of spiritual reality, the need to perceive it again through the agency of his senses remains fully alive in him. Just as a roundly developed person interested in achieving a full experience of reality awakens, as a result of perceiving with his senses, to a longing to perceive the complementing world of elemental beings so, in turn, does a person perceiving them long for the complementing content of sensory perception.

In the totality of human life, the spirit calls for the senses and the senses for the spirit. There would be emptiness in spiritual existence if sensory experience were not represented there in the form of memories, and sensory experience would be darkened if the power of the spirit were not raying light into it, even though there is only subconscious awareness of this fact.

When an individual has matured to the point of sharing the experience of Michael's activity, there will be no impoverishment of soul in his experience of nature, but instead an enrichment. His feeling life will not tend to withdraw from sensory experience, but rather to be joyously inclined to take up into his being all the wonders of the world of the senses.

*

GUIDELINES

1. The human sense organization does not belong to man himself; it is rather a system built into him by the surrounding world in the course of his lifetime on the earth.

Spatially, the eye is part of him, but in its inner nature it is part of the world. Man projects his soul-spiritual being into what the world is experiencing in him through the agency of his senses. He does not absorb into himself aspects of his physical environment while living on earth. Rather does his soul-spiritual being grow into his surroundings.

2. A similar situation prevails with respect to his thinking organization. He grows into the life of the stars through its possession, and comes to know himself as a star world. He lives and moves and has his being in universal thoughts when, in the experience of knowledge, he has divested himself of his sense organization.

3. Upon divesting himself of both the earthly world and the starry universe, he confronts himself as a soul-spiritual being. Here he is no longer world, but, in the true sense, man. To become aware of his experience in this state means self-knowledge, just as becoming aware in his sense and thinking organizations means knowledge of the world.

XXVI
MEMORY AND CONSCIENCE

Man gives himself up to the cosmos when he sleeps. He takes back to it what lived in him as the fruit of former earthly lives when he descended to earth from the soul-spiritual world. This content of his essential being is withdrawn from the cosmos in his waking hours.

Life between birth and death runs its course in this rhythmical alternation between giving himself up to the cosmos and withdrawing from it.

Man's withdrawal from the cosmos is accompanied by a simultaneous absorption of his soul-spiritual being into his nerve-sense organization. The physical and life processes taking place in that organization join forces with the soul-spiritual element of waking man in a unified functioning, which includes sensory perception, the forming of memory pictures, and the life of fantasy. All these functions are attached to the physical body. To man's thinking organization are attached his mental images and his experience of thinking, functions in which he experiences consciously what lived in him semi-consciously as perception, memory and fantasy.

This thinking organization includes the realm from which man obtains his experience of self-awareness. The thinking organization is a star organization. If it were to restrict its life to this alone, however, human beings would not be possessors of self-consciousness, but of an awareness of the gods. But the thinking organization is a star organization withdrawn from the starry universe and transplanted into the scene of earth events. In that man experiences this star world in the terrestrial sphere, he becomes a self-aware being.

So we have here that region of man's inner life in which the divine-spiritual world bound up with the human race sets man free so that he can become a human being in the fullest sense.

But immediately below the level of the thinking organization, the level at which sensory perception, the forming of mental images, and memory take place, the divine-spiritual world participates in the life lived by human beings. The divine-spiritual may be said to live in man's development of memory while he is in the waking state. For the related functions of sensory perception and fantasy are simply modifications of the memory forming function. In sensory perception the forming of the content of memory is just in the beginning phase, whereas in the content of fantasy there lights up in the soul what it retains in its inner life of memory content.

The sleeping state carries the soul-spiritual in man over into the cosmos. He is immersed in the divine-spiritual world with his astral and ego activities. Not only is he outside the physical world, he is outside the starry world as well. But he is within the divine-spiritual beings to whom he owes his existence.

In the present epoch of cosmic evolution, these divine-spiritual beings are active, imprinting on man's astral body and ego during sleep the moral content of the universe. Everything of a cosmic nature that goes on in man while he is asleep is true moral action, action not in any sense similar to what transpires in nature.

Man carries over from his sleeping into his waking state the after-effects of this activity. These effects remain dormant since man is awake only in that part of his life that tends in the direction of the realm of thinking. What actually goes on in the sphere of his will is just as swathed in obscurity while he is awake as is his entire soul life while he sleeps. But the divine-spiritual goes on working in his sleeping will life even while he is in the waking state. Man is morally as virtuous or the opposite as it is possible for him to be, measured by how close he is able to come to the divine-spiritual beings during sleep. He comes closer to, or remains further removed from them in accordance with the moral orientation of his previous earthly lives.

There sounds forth out of the depths of man's waking soul being what was implanted in it through his association with the divine-spiritual world during his sleep. What sounds forth is the voice of conscience.

So we see how something that a materialistic outlook tends to explain naturalistically is a moral matter to spiritual science.

The divine-spiritual works directly in the memory of the waking human being, whereas it works indirectly, as an after-effect, in his conscience when he is in the waking state.

The forming of memory pictures goes on in the nerve-sense system. The building of conscience runs its course as a purely soul-spiritual process, but within the metabolic-limb system.

Between these two lies the rhythmic system, its activity developed to link these polar opposites. As the breathing rhythm, it is in intimate connection with sensory perception and with thinking. This process is coarsest in lung breathing; it undergoes refinement, and, as a refined breathing process, becomes thinking and sensory perception. The latter is indeed close to breathing, but it is a breathing that makes use of the sense organs rather than the lungs. Still more remote from lung breathing is the process of forming mental images and thinking, both functions being supported by the thinking organization. What borders on the rhythm of the circulation of the blood and may be called an internal form of breathing connected with the metabolic-limb system is seen in the activity of fantasy, which extends as a soul function into the will sphere just as the rhythm of the circulation of the blood extends into the metabolic-limb system.

The thinking organization comes close to the will organization in the exercise of fantasy; here, while awake, an individual steeps himself in his sleep sphere. That is why the contents of the souls of individuals so organized appear like waking dreams. Goethe's was a nature of this kind. It caused him to say that Schiller had to interpret his poetic dreams.

We find the opposite kind of nature in Schiller. He lived

155

on the strength of what he brought with him from previous incarnations. He had to search for a fantasy content for his energetic will.

Individuals with a predisposition to the fantasy sphere, such that the contemplation of sensory reality conjures up involuntary fantasy pictures in them, are counted on by the Ahrimanic powers in their world planning. They think that with the help of this type of human being they will be able to make a complete break with the past in human evolution and to steer it in the direction they desire.

Lucifer counts on individuals who are organized toward the will sphere but who turn sensory contemplation into fantasy pictures out of an inner enthusiasm for an idealistic world conception. Lucifer wants to use people of this kind to keep human evolution governed wholly by impulses from the past. He could then save mankind from entering the sphere where Ahriman's power must be overcome.

In his existence on the earth, man occupies a position between two polar opposites. Stars spread out above him. From these ray the forces connected with everything calculable and regular. The regular alternation of day and night; of the seasons, and of other longer time periods is the earthly mirroring of what goes on in the starry heavens.

The opposite pole sends out its rays from the center of the earth. Irregularity is the rule here. Wind and weather, thunder and lightning, earthquakes, volcanic outbursts, all these reflect this inner earthly activity.

Man is an image of this star-earth reality. A starry order lives in his thinking organization, earthly chaos in his limb will organization. Man's earthly being is experienced in the free balance of the rhythmic system.

*

GUIDELINES

1. Man's organization as a bodily and spiritual being occurs from two sides. The first is the physical and etheric cos-

mos. What rays into this organization of man's being from the divine-spiritual world lives in him as the capacity of sensory perception, the faculty of memory, and the activity of fantasy.

2. The second is the organization man receives from his earlier incarnations. This organization is of a wholly soul-spiritual nature and lives in man through the agency of his astral body and his ego. The activity of divine-spiritual beings living into man's human being flashes up in him as the voice of conscience and all that is attached to it.

3. Man has in his rhythmic organization the constant interplay of the two aspects of divine-spiritual impulses. In the experience of rhythm, the faculty of memory is carried over into will reality, the power of conscience into the realm of man's life of ideas.

XXVII

THE APPARENT EXTINGUISHING
OF SPIRITUAL KNOWLEDGE IN MODERN TIMES

Anyone desirous of forming a correct idea of Anthroposophy's relationship to the development of the consciousness soul will need to look again and again at the state of mind of cultured peoples that made its first appearance at the dawning of the scientific outlook and reached a peak in the nineteenth century.

Let us consider the nature of this period and compare it with that of other epochs.

Throughout the whole extent of conscious human evolution, learning was regarded as the element that brought man and the spiritual world together. A man's relationship to the spiritual was thought of as the product of knowledge. In art and religion, knowledge lived.

This changed when the consciousness-soul age began to dawn. Learning came to be little concerned with a large part of man's soul life. It preferred to investigate what developed as the relationship man has to existence when he is training his senses and critical judgment on the world of 'nature.' It felt no further desire to concern itself with what he developed as a relationship to the spiritual world when he applied his powers of inner perception to it in the same way that he applied his senses.

So the necessity arose to link man's spiritual life to learning of the past, to tradition, rather than to learning of the present day.

Human soul life was thus split in half. Man's glance fell, on the one side, on natural science as this developed in the living present and spread over more and more areas. On the other side was the experiencing of a relationship to the Spiritual world nourished in earlier times by an appropriate learning. All understanding as to how knowledge of this kind came to be in those earlier times was gradually lost. Traditions were still there, but the path on which truths thus handed down had become knowledge was no longer accessible. People could only believe in the traditions that remained.

A person of the mid-nineteenth century who contemplated the spiritual situation with a clear perspective would have had to say that mankind had come to believe itself capable of producing only the kind of knowledge that has nothing to do with the spirit; that an earlier humanity had been able to investigate what it was possible to know about the spiritual, but that this ability had been lost to human souls.

The full significance of what mankind thus actually faced went unrealized. People were content with the statement that knowledge simply cannot reach as high as to the spiritual world, and that it can therefore be only a matter of belief.

Let us try to gain a clearer understanding of this fact by examining the period in which Greek wisdom was giving way to a Christianized Rome. When the last schools of Greek philosophy were closed by Caesar, the last custodians of ancient wisdom left the region where Europe's spiritual life was developing. They found asylum in the Academy of Gondishapur in Asia. This was one of the places in the Orient where, as a result of Alexander's deeds, ancient learning had been preserved, and it lived on at Gondishapur in the form given it by Aristotle.

But that oriental stream that can be termed Arabism seized upon it. One aspect of Arabism was that it was a premature development of the consciousness soul. In the fact that the life of the soul was moving prematurely in the consciousness-soul direction, Arabism made it possible for a spiritual wave to surge from Asia over Africa and southern and western Europe, filling certain Europeans with an intellectuality that should have come as a later development. In the seventh and eighth centuries, southern and western Europe were the recipients of spiritual impulses the coming of which should have waited for the consciousness-soul age.

This spiritual wave was capable of awakening the intellectual element in man, but it could not bring about the deeper experience necessary for entering the spiritual world.

So when a man in the period of the fifteenth to the nineteenth centuries bestirred himself to acquire knowledge, he could penetrate only to a certain depth that did not suffice to reach the spiritual realm.

The Arabism infiltrating European spiritual life kept learning far removed from the world of the spirit. It brought premature stimulation to intellects incapable of grasping anything beyond external nature.

This Arabism proved itself indeed powerful. Individuals caught up in it began to be laid hold on by an inner arrogance, which was largely subconscious. They did indeed feel the power of intellectualism, but not mere intellect's incapacity to penetrate reality. So they abandoned themselves to the external facts presented to their senses without any effort on their part, but it did not occur to them to search for spiritual reality.

Such was the situation confronting the spiritual life of the Middle Ages, which had inherited a vast legacy of traditions concerning the spiritual world. But the soul life of the time was so impregnated with intellectualism by the Arabism at work behind the scenes, as it were, that learning had no access to the sources from which the content of these traditions issued.

From the Middle Ages on, a battle raged between what people felt instinctively to be a connection with the spiritual and the shape thinking had assumed under the influence of Arabism.

People sensed the world of ideas within them; it was experienced as a most real presence. But they did not feel themselves in possession of the power to experience the spiritual in ideas. This gave rise to Realism, which sensed the reality in ideas but could not find it. Realism discerned the sounding of the World Word in the world of ideas, but was incapable of understanding its language.

Nominalism, its philosophic opponent, denied the very fact of the sounding because of a failure to understand it. To Nominalism, the world of ideas was just a set of formulas in the human soul, lacking any basis in spiritual reality.

The tempestuous battling of these streams continued to be felt right down to the nineteenth century. Nominalism became the mode of thinking of the natural sciences. It built up an impressive system of concepts of the world of the senses, but wiped out insight into the nature of the world of ideas. Realism lived a dead existence. It knew that the world of ideas was real, but could not rise to it in living knowledge.

We will attain to this if Anthroposophy finds the way from ideas to a spiritual experience in ideas. A truly matured Realism must come to the aid of natural scientific Nominalism, providing a path of insight that will prove that knowledge of the spirit has not been extinguished among men, but can instead rise, refreshed from the fount of recently developed soul capacities, to re-enter human evolution in a new ascent.

*

GUIDELINES

1. A depressing perspective presents itself to those who contemplate the evolution of mankind in the present scientific age. Knowledge of everything pertaining to the external world is nothing short of brilliant. But, also, man's consciousness is such as to rule out any possibility of attaining knowledge of the spiritual world.

2. It appears as though this kind of insight was accessible to man in earlier times only, and that we must, therefore, re-

main satisfied with the possession of ancient traditions, making them objects of belief.

3. A lack of belief in the spiritual content of ideas, arising in the Middle Ages from uncertainty as to man's relationship to the spiritual world, gave rise to Nominalism. Its continuation into the present is the basis of modern science. Realism came into being as knowledge of the reality of ideas, but this philosophic approach can come to fulfillment only through Anthroposophy.

XXVIII

THE HISTORIC UPHEAVALS ATTENDANT
UPON THE BIRTH OF THE CONSCIOUSNESS SOUL

The downfall of the Roman Empire accompanied by the appearance on the scene of peoples coming from the East in the so-called Great Migration is a historic phenomenon that calls for ongoing scrutiny and investigation because there continued to be many after-effects of these shattering events.

But it is not possible for external historical contemplation to arrive at an understanding of these particular occurrences. For that, the souls of the peoples involved in the migrations and in the downfall of the Roman Empire must be taken into account.

Greek and Roman civilization flourished during the period when the intellectual soul was developing in the human race. Indeed, the Greeks and Romans were the true carriers of this development. But in their case the development of this stage of soul did not have within it the germinal power to generate the consciousness soul out of itself. Everything of a soul and spiritual content stored in the intellectual soul poured out in living fullness in Greek and Roman civilization. But it could not flow over of its own strength into the consciousness soul.

Despite this, the consciousness soul, of course, appeared when the right moment came. But it did so in a way indicating that the consciousness soul was not born as a product of the Greek and Roman personality, but was instead implanted in it from without.

The state of union with divine-spiritual beings and the later detachment from them so often referred to in these contemplations vary in intensity with the passage of time. In earlier epochs, powerful effects were felt in human evolution in the form of stirring events. There was less intensity in the experiencing of the Greeks and Romans during the first Christian centuries. While they were involved in fully developing the intellectual soul in their own natures, the Greeks and Romans had a significant, if unconscious, feeling of being detached from divine-spiritual being and of their humanness becoming independent. This ceased to be the case in the first Christian centuries. The waxing tide of the consciousness soul was experienced as union with the divine-spiritual. There was a retrogressive development from a greater to a lesser independence of soul. The content of Christianity could not be taken up by man's consciousness soul for the reason that this soul itself could not be absorbed by human nature.

This Christian content was therefore felt to be something given from without by the external spiritual world rather than as an element that one could grow together with as a result of exercising one's own cognitive powers.

The situation was different in the case of peoples appearing on the historical scene from the northeast. They had passed through the intellectual soul stage in a state of being experienced by them as dependence on the spiritual world. They only began to have some sense of human independence when the first forces of the consciousness soul were putting in an appearance in early Christian times. In their case, the consciousness soul was experienced as something quite bound up with human nature. They felt a joyous inner strength developing in them as the consciousness soul came alive within them.

The content of Christianity was taken up into the burgeoning life of the dawning consciousness soul among these peoples. They sensed it as something coming to life within their souls rather than as something given from without.

This was the state of mind in which these peoples approached the Roman Empire and everything connected with it. It was the mood of Arianism as contrasted with Atha-

166

nasianism. With these, a profound inner division made itself felt in world historical evolution.

A divine-spiritual element, which was not fully bound up with life on earth but which merely sent its rays into it, was at work in the more external consciousness soul of the Greeks and Romans, whereas there was still only a weak influence on the consciousness soul of the Franks and Germans and related peoples, emanating from as much of the divine-spiritual as was able to relate itself to human nature.

The next thing that happened was that the Christian content living in the consciousness soul as it hovered over man was widely disseminated. As much of this content as had united itself with the soul remained within it as an incentive, an impulse, waiting for a further development that can occur only when the consciousness soul has reached a certain point in its evolution.

The period from the first Christian centuries down to the consciousness-soul age was one in which a spiritual content hovered over mankind, dominating its spiritual life—a content with which man could not connect himself for purposes of knowledge. He therefore established an external connection with it. He "explained" it and mulled over the problem of how inadequate the forces of the soul were to make a thinking connection with it. He drew a distinction between the realms accessible to knowledge and those that were not. He abandoned any effort to activate soul forces that might lift him in cognition to the spiritual world. So there came a time, at the turn of the seventeenth and eighteenth centuries, when he turned entirely away from the soul forces focused on spiritual concerns, from a cognitional approach to the spirit, and began to live only in soul forces focused on what the senses perceive.

Man's cognitive powers became dullest where spiritual matters were concerned, especially in the eighteenth century.

Thinkers lost the spiritual content of their ideas. In the Idealism of the first half of the nineteenth century they advanced these same ideas, so empty of all spirit, as the creative world content; Fichte, Schelling and Hegel were among them. Or else they called attention to a supersensible element that disappeared into thin air because it had no trace of the spirit left in it. Spencer and John Stuart Mill are examples. Their ideas are dead because they did not seek the living spirit.

The spiritual organ for perceiving the spiritual element was wholly lost.

It was no longer possible to travel the old path of spiritual insight. Soul forces harboring the developing consciousness soul within them must seek out a renewed, living, elemental and direct relationship with the spiritual world. It is Anthroposophy's intention to strive toward that goal.

The leading personalities of our period are the very ones who do not understand what this intention is, with the result that the circles around them are also kept away from Anthroposophy. These leading figures live with a soul content that has gradually lost the habit of making use of any spiritual powers whatsoever. They take the attitude that a person with a paralyzed organ is being asked to use it, since man's higher cognitional powers were indeed paralyzed in the period from the sixteenth to the middle of the nineteenth century. Humanity was totally unaware that this was happening and it regarded the one-sided directing of cognition upon the sensory world as a great advance.

*

GUIDELINES

1. The Greeks and Romans were the peoples with a special predisposition to intellectual-soul development, and they brought this stage of the soul to complete maturity. But they were not gifted with a germinal capacity to go straight on to the consciousness-soul stage. Their soul life was wholly swallowed up by and submerged in the intellectual soul.

2. But during the period beginning with the birth of Christianity and lasting into the age of consciousness-soul development, there reigns a world of the spirit that does not link itself with human soul forces. Although the latter "explain" the spiritual world, they have no actual experience of it.

3. There lived in the peoples of the Great Migration who swarmed over the Roman Empire from the northeast a grasp, imbued with feeling, of the intellectual soul. The consciousness soul rooted in that feeling element, however, developed in their soul being. Their inner life waited expectantly for the time to come when a uniting of the soul with the spiritual world would again become possible.

XXIX
FROM NATURE TO SUB-NATURE

People say that the philosophic age was brought to a close in the middle of the nineteenth century with the coming into its own of the age of natural science. They say that the natural-scientific age is still in full swing, although many assert their belief that a revival of certain aspects of philosophy is to be observed.

All this corresponds to recent developments in the pursuit of knowledge, but not with the ways of life itself. Man still lives with his mental picturing in the world of nature, even though he brings a mechanistic way of thinking to its understanding. But, where his will life is concerned, he lives to such a great extent in the mechanics of the technological process that this has long since given the scientific era a brand-new nuance.

Human life must be looked at from two sides if we are to understand it. Man brings with him from past incarnations the capacity to form pictures of the cosmic influences working in from the earth's environment and of those at work within the earthly realm. His senses perceive the effects of cosmic influences on the earth, and his thinking organization thinks the cosmic element that acts upon the earth from its environment.

So he lives in perception through the agency of his physical body, and in thinking through the etheric body.

What goes on in his astral body and in his ego runs its course in more hidden soul realms, as, for example, in destiny. But it should be looked for in the elementary, simple life processes rather than in destiny's complex workings.

Man connects himself with certain forces of the earth when he subjects his organism to these forces. He learns to

171

stand upright and to walk; he learns to relate himself with his hands and arms to the balance of earthly forces.

These forces are not of the kind that works in from the cosmos; they are rather purely terrestrial.

Nothing that man experiences is actually an abstraction. He simply does not understand where the experience came from, and therefore fabricates abstractions out of his ideas about the real. He talks of the laws of mechanics and believes that he has abstracted them from nature. That is not the case, however; everything that he has experienced in the way of purely mechanical laws comes from an inner experiencing of his own orientation in relation to the earthly sphere; that is, in his stance, his walking, and so on.

This marks the mechanical element as purely earthly. But the laws of nature relating to color, tone, etc., came to the earth from out of the cosmos, and only in the earthly realm was the mechanical element also implanted into this complex of natural laws, just as man only encounters it in his own personal experience while on earth.

By far the greater part of the effects of technology on civilization and the far-reaching involvement with it of human life derive not from nature but from sub-nature—a world emancipated from nature in a downward direction.

We should note how Orientals in search of the spiritual try to liberate themselves from merely earthly states of balance. When engaged in meditation, they assume a position that brings them into a purely cosmic balance, a position in which the earth no longer exercises an influence on the orientation of the organism. (This is said only in order to clarify the above, not to suggest imitation. Those familiar with my writings know how eastern and western practices differ in this respect.)

Human beings needed this relationship to the purely earthly for their consciousness-soul development. That brought about the tendency everywhere in recent times to implement through their doing all the experiences with which they now had to become familiar. They encountered the Ahrimanic element in their immersion in the purely earthly, and had to find the right relationship of their own beings to it.

But thus far the possibility of finding the right relationship to the Ahrimanic civilization of the technological era has escaped them. Man has got to find the strength, the inner cognitive power, to avoid being overwhelmed by Ahriman in the technological civilization of the present. Sub-nature must be grasped for what it is, and this can happen only if man rises at least as high above nature in a cosmic direction in pursuit of spiritual insight as he has descended with his technology to a sub-natural level. Our age requires a form of knowledge rising above nature because it has to deal with a life content of dangerous potential that has sunk below the level of the natural. To say this is certainly not to advocate a return to earlier cultural phases, but rather to indicate that man should find the way to bring the new state of culture into right relationship to himself and to the cosmos.

Few individuals are aware today of the significant spiritual tasks that are in the making here for the human race. Electricity, which was hailed at the time of its discovery as the soul of the natural world, must be recognized in its real nature as a force that leads from nature to sub-nature. Man must not let himself be dragged down with it.

In ages before a technology divorced from what we may properly call nature had come into existence, man found the spirit in contemplating nature. The detaching of technology fixed his attention on the mechanistic-material as the element on which he would henceforth focus his scientific efforts. Everything of a divine-spiritual nature connected with the wellsprings of mankind's evolution is absent here. The purely Ahrimanic rules this sphere.

In spiritual science a sphere is created that has no trace of an Ahrimanic element in it. It is precisely through the receptive understanding of that spirituality to which the Ahrimanic powers have no access, that man will find the strength to meet and confront Ahriman in the world.

*

GUIDELINES

1. In the age of natural science that began about the middle of the nineteenth century, men's cultural activities slid gradually, not only into the lowest depths of nature, but beneath nature. Technology led into a sub-natural realm.

2. This makes it necessary for man to cultivate experience of spiritual insight in which he is elevated as far above nature as he sinks below it when he occupies himself with the sub-natural realm of technology. To do this enables him to create sufficient strength to keep from being submerged.

3. An earlier view of nature still harbored within it the spirit with which the wellsprings of mankind's evolution are bound up. This spirit gradually disappeared from the way nature was regarded, and a purely Ahrimanic spirit pervaded it and flowed from it into the technological civilization that developed.